jQuery UI Cookbook

70 recipes to create responsive and engaging user interfaces in jQuery

Adam Boduch

BIRMINGHAM - MUMBAI

jQuery UI Cookbook

First published: July 2013

Production Reference: 1120713

Published by Packt Publishing Ltd.
Livery Place
35 Livery Street
Birmingham B3 2PB, UK.

ISBN 978-1-78216-218-6

www.packtpub.com

Cover Image by Jarek Blaminsky (milak6@wp.pl)

Credits

Author
Adam Boduch

Reviewers
Hrishikesh Choudhari

Deepak Vohra

Acquisition Editor
Edward Gordon

Lead Technical Editor
Susmita Panda

Technical Editors
Shashank Desai

Worrell Lewis

Rikita Poojari

Amit Ramadas

Project Coordinator
Kranti Berde

Proofreaders
Lydia May Morris

Jonathan Todd

Indexer
Monica Ajmera Mehta

Production Coordinator
Aditi Gajjar

Cover Work
Aditi Gajjar

About the Author

Adam Boduch has spent the last several years developing user interfaces for large-scale software systems. Starting out as a backend Python developer, he was lured to the frontend by tools like jQuery UI. Adam is passionate about readable code, and writes extensively about jQuery UI widgets, including his previous book *jQuery UI Themes Beginner's Guide, Packt Publishing*.

When Adam isn't coding, reading or writing, you will usually find him playing hockey, or spending time with his family.

About the Reviewers

Hrishikesh Choudhari has been developing single page rich applications using a host of client-side technologies. He has a special preference for JSON-emitting servers and delicious interfaces on the frontend. He has worked on the backend for innovative social networks.

He is a professional data visualization expert, and builds his own visualization micro libraries for SVG. He contributed to the book *FusionCharts Beginner's Guide, Packt Publishing*. He also helped design dashboards for clients ranging from Fortune 10 companies to startups.

He works on his skills to be a full stack web architect. He graduated magna cum laude in B.S. in Software Engineering from Champlain College, USA.

In his free time, he speed-reads, cooks, and goes for long walks. You can follow him on Twitter at `@hchoudhari` or on LinkedIn `in.linkedin.com/in/hrishikeshchoudhari`. His website can be found at `http://hrishikeshchoudhari.com/`.

Deepak Vohra is a consultant and a principal member of the NuBean.com software company. He is a Sun Certified Java Programmer and Web Component Developer, and has worked in the fields of XML and Java programming and J2EE for over five years. He is the co-author of the book *Pro XML Development with Java Technology, Apress*, and was the technical reviewer for the book *WebLogic: The Definitive Guide, O'Reilly Media*.

Deepak was also the technical reviewer for the book *Ruby Programming for the Absolute Beginner, Course Technology PTR* and the Technical Editor for the book *Prototype and Scriptaculous in Action, Manning Publications*. He is also the author of the books *JDBC 4.0 and Oracle JDeveloper for J2EE Development, Processing XML Documents with Oracle JDeveloper 11g*, and *EJB 3.0 Database Persistence with Oracle Fusion Middleware 11g, Packt Publishing*.

www.PacktPub.com

Support files, eBooks, discount offers and more

You might want to visit www.PacktPub.com for support files and downloads related to your book.

Did you know that Packt offers eBook versions of every book published, with PDF and ePub files available? You can upgrade to the eBook version at www.PacktPub.com and as a print book customer, you are entitled to a discount on the eBook copy. Get in touch with us at service@packtpub.com for more details.

At www.PacktPub.com, you can also read a collection of free technical articles, sign up for a range of free newsletters and receive exclusive discounts and offers on Packt books and eBooks.

http://PacktLib.PacktPub.com

Do you need instant solutions to your IT questions? PacktLib is Packt's online digital book library. Here, you can access, read and search across Packt's entire library of books.

Why Subscribe?

- ► Fully searchable across every book published by Packt
- ► Copy and paste, print and bookmark content
- ► On demand and accessible via web browser

Free Access for Packt account holders

If you have an account with Packt at www.PacktPub.com, you can use this to access PacktLib today and view nine entirely free books. Simply use your login credentials for immediate access.

For Ted

Table of Contents

Preface

Creating user experiences that excite users is a fun and rewarding job. You're essentially improving the lives of many people. Most UI developers have their eye on the finish line, seeing their product put to use. The faster we get to that finish line without sacrificing quality, the better. The tools we use to help get us there can make all the difference in the world.

Part of what makes the jQuery Framework so popular among developers, the "write less, do more" mantra, materializes in jQuery UI as well. The modern versions of HTML and CSS standards have the tools required for assembling a robust, responsive user interface. Where this idea falls apart—browser inconsistencies and lack of development conventions and patterns across projects—jQuery UI steps in. The goal of jQuery UI isn't to reinvent the way we write web applications, but rather, to fill in gaps and progressively enhance existing browser components.

Like any framework, jQuery UI isn't for everyone, nor is it perfect for those that do use it. The framework embraces this fact, and provides extensibility mechanisms for most situations you might find yourself in. My goal with this book is to share with you some experiences I've had with jQuery UI widgets. I've extended where possible, and hacked where necessary. I'm sure you'll find the majority of the recipes in this book useful, no matter what kind of application you're building.

What this book covers

Chapter 1, Creating Accordions, helps you learn how to drag-and-drop between accordion widgets. In addition, you'll learn how to extend the accordion theme.

Chapter 2, Including Autocompletes, explains the autocomplete widget that shows how to use multiple data sources. Turning select options into autocomplete widgets, and remote data source filtering are covered too.

Chapter 3, Crafting Buttons, explains about modifying buttons for our application. Buttons can be simple, modifying text and icon options. Or, buttons can be more involved, such as when working with button sets. We'll look into spacing issues, and how to apply effects.

Chapter 4, Developing Datepickers, talks about datepicker, which is the most widely-used widget, yet the most under-utilized. We'll uncover some potentials of the widget by using some techniques to better integrate datepicker into your application.

Chapter 5, Adding Dialogs, discusses dialog widgets, which often rely on API data. We'll look into loading data and dialog display issues. We also cover changing the dialog title bar, and applying effects to the widget.

Chapter 6, Making Menus, helps you learn how to make sortable menu items. We'll address theme concerns and highlighting the active menu item as well.

Chapter 7, Progress Bars, shows how to add labels to progress bars. We'll also extend the progress bar to make a loading widget.

Chapter 8, Using Sliders, talks about the slider widget that doesn't display step increments. Here, you will extend the widget to provide this capability. We also look into changing the visual display of the slider handle.

Chapter 9, Using Spinners, explains spinners, which are often used in forms. So we deal with formatting spinner values for local currencies and dates in this chapter. We'll also look into addressing theme concerns with the widget.

Chapter 10, Using Tabs, introduces some new techniques in working with tabs, that is, using each tab as a plain URL link. We also cover some more advanced tab navigation usage—dynamic loading and reading the browser hash.

Chapter 11, Using Tooltips, explains tooltips, which can be applied to just about anything on the page. In this chapter, we'll show you how to apply effects to the tooltip, change the tooltip state, and apply tooltips to selected text.

Chapter 12, Widgets and More!, talks about widgets, which don't exist in a vacuum. They're part of a larger application. This chapter covers the bigger jQuery UI development picture. This includes building a widget from scratch, building your own development tools, and working with Backbone.

What you need for this book

You will require the following:

- A modern web browser for running the examples.
- A text-editor for reading along and tweaking the examples.
- All JavaScript dependencies included in the examples download.
- Python (optional); some examples require a web server, and use the built-in Python web server in the examples. The examples could use any web server with the appropriate adjustments.

Who this book is for

This book is for the jQuery UI developer looking to improve their existing applications, extract ideas for their new application, or to better understand the overall widget architecture. The reader should at least have a rudimentary understanding of what jQuery UI is, and have written some code that uses jQuery UI. The recipes in this book are targeted at the intermediate jQuery UI developer. Depending on your needs, each recipe is self-contained enough to be useful on its own, but connected enough to guide you to others.

Conventions

In this book, you will find a number of styles of text that distinguish between different kinds of information. Here are some examples of these styles, and an explanation of their meaning.

Code words in text are shown as follows: "In this scenario, we're better off just changing the default dateFormat value to something our application uses throughout."

A block of code is set as follows:

```
$(function() {
    $( ".calendar" ).datepicker();
});
```

New terms and **important words** are shown in bold. Words that you see on the screen, in menus or dialog boxes for example, appear in the text like this: " Clicking on the **no icons** link would result in the button icons being removed, and replaced with their text."

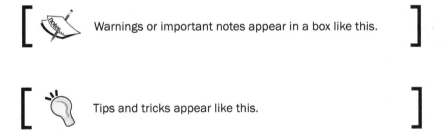

> Warnings or important notes appear in a box like this.

> Tips and tricks appear like this.

Reader feedback

Feedback from our readers is always welcome. Let us know what you think about this book—what you liked or may have disliked. Reader feedback is important for us to develop titles that you really get the most out of.

To send us general feedback, simply send an e-mail to `feedback@packtpub.com`, and mention the book title via the subject of your message.

If there is a topic that you have expertise in and you are interested in either writing or contributing to a book, see our author guide on `www.packtpub.com/authors`.

Customer support

Now that you are the proud owner of a Packt book, we have a number of things to help you to get the most from your purchase.

Downloading the example code

You can download the example code files for all Packt books you have purchased from your account at `http://www.packtpub.com`. If you purchased this book elsewhere, you can visit `http://www.packtpub.com/support` and register to have the files e-mailed directly to you.

Errata

Although we have taken every care to ensure the accuracy of our content, mistakes do happen. If you find a mistake in one of our books—maybe a mistake in the text or the code—we would be grateful if you would report this to us. By doing so, you can save other readers from frustration and help us improve subsequent versions of this book. If you find any errata, please report them by visiting `http://www.packtpub.com/submit-errata`, selecting your book, clicking on the **errata submission form** link, and entering the details of your errata. Once your errata are verified, your submission will be accepted and the errata will be uploaded on our website, or added to any list of existing errata, under the Errata section of that title. Any existing errata can be viewed by selecting your title from `http://www.packtpub.com/support`.

Piracy

Piracy of copyright material on the Internet is an ongoing problem across all media. At Packt, we take the protection of our copyright and licenses very seriously. If you come across any illegal copies of our works, in any form, on the Internet, please provide us with the location address or website name immediately so that we can pursue a remedy.

Please contact us at `copyright@packtpub.com` with a link to the suspected pirated material.

We appreciate your help in protecting our authors, and our ability to bring you valuable content.

Questions

You can contact us at `questions@packtpub.com` if you are having a problem with any aspect of the book, and we will do our best to address it.

1

Creating Accordions

In this chapter, we will cover the following recipes:

- ► Section navigation using the Tab key
- ► Dynamically changing the height style
- ► Resizable content sections
- ► Controlling spacing with themes
- ► Sorting accordion sections
- ► Dragging-and-dropping between accordions

Introduction

In this chapter, we will explore the various ways in which we can extend the **accordion** widget to accommodate a number of scenarios. The accordion widget offers a lot of out-of-the-box functionality. For example, without any configuration, we get a themed container widget that groups contents into sections.

We'll focus on use cases that shed light on the inner workings of the accordion widget. Keyboard events are one way to navigate the page, and we can enhance the accordion's support for these events. Some magic happens behind the scene to come up with each section's height, when expanded. We'll see how we can work with these configurations, especially when the section height changes on the fly.

Also on the topic of height, we can let the user control the height of individual sections, or, from a theme perspective, we can control the space between the accordion components. Finally, we'll look at some of the more advanced accordion usage where we give the user the freedom to sort their accordion sections and to drag sections from one accordion to another.

Section navigation using the Tab key

In most desktop environments, the *Tab* key is a secret weapon in navigation—one tool that many users are accustomed to. Likewise, we can utilize the *Tab* key in HTML5 applications using the `tabindex` property. This tells the browser the order in which to focus elements, each time the key is pressed.

Unfortunately, this isn't as straightforward as it looks with accordion widgets. We can't specify a `tabindex` value in each section header and expect the *Tab* key events to work as expected. Instead, the default widget implementation provides a different kind of key navigation—the *up* and *down* arrow keys. Ideally, it would be useful to give users the ability to navigate through the accordion sections using the *Tab* key that they're familiar with, while preserving the default key navigation provided by the widget.

Getting ready

To get started, we'll want a basic accordion; ideally, something simple that has basic content within each section, so that we can visually see how the *Tab* key behavior works before we implement custom events, and afterward.

As a guide, here is my basic accordion markup:

```
<div id="accordion">
    <h3>Section 1</h3>
    <div>
        <p>Section 1 content</p>
    </div>
    <h3>Section 2</h3>
    <div>
        <p>Section 2 content</p>
    </div>
    <h3>Section 3</h3>
    <div>
        <p>Section 3 content</p>
    </div>
    <h3>Section 4</h3>
    <div>
        <p>Section 4 content</p>
    </div>
</div>
```

And, here is the code used to instantiate the accordion widget:

```
$(function() {

    $( "#accordion" ).accordion({
        collapsible: true
    });

});
```

Downloading the example code

You can download the example code files for all Packt books you have purchased from your account at http://www.packtpub.com. If you purchased this book elsewhere, you can visit http://www.packtpub.com/support and register to have the files e-mailed directly to you.

We now have a basic collapsible accordion widget that we can look at in the browser. The reason we're adding the collapsible option here is so that we can experiment with the key navigation—we get a better view of which section is in focus when all are collapsed. You can see how the *up* and *down* arrow keys allow the user to traverse through the accordion sections while the *Tab* key has no effect. Let's change that.

How to do it...

We're going to extend the accordion widget to include an event handler for keypress events. The default accordion implementation has keypress events for dealing with the *up*, *down*, *left*, *right*, and *Enter* keys. We don't need to change that. Instead, we add our own handler that understands what to do when the *Tab* key and *Shift + Tab* keys are pressed.

Look at the following code:

```
(function( $, undefined ) {

$.widget( "ab.accordion", $.ui.accordion, {

    _create: function () {

        this._super( "_create" );
        this._on( this.headers, { keydown: "_tabkeydown" } );

    },
```

```javascript
_tabkeydown: function ( event ) {

    if ( event.altKey || event.ctrlKey ) {
        return;
     }

    if ( event.keyCode !== $.ui.keyCode.TAB ) {
        return;
    }

    var headers = this.headers,
        headerLength = headers.length,
        headerIndex = headers.index( event.target ),
        toFocus = false;

    if ( event.shiftKey && headerIndex - 1 >= 0 ) {
        toFocus = headers[ headerIndex - 1 ];
    }

    if ( !event.shiftKey && headerIndex + 1 < headerLength ) {
        toFocus = headers[ headerIndex + 1 ];
    }

    if ( toFocus ) {

        $( event.target ).attr( "tabIndex", -1 );
        $( toFocus ).attr( "tabIndex", 0 );
        toFocus.focus();
        event.preventDefault();

    }

 }

});

})( jQuery );

$(function() {

    $( "#accordion" ).accordion({
        collapsible: true
    });

});
```

How it works...

We're creating a new accordion widget here by extending the default accordion widget. The advantage to this approach of extending the accordion widget is that we're not tinkering with instances of the widget; all accordion instances will acquire this new behavior.

The `_create()` method is replaced with our new implementation of it. The first thing we do in this replacement method is call the original `_create()` method. We don't want to prevent the default setup actions of the accordion widget from taking place. So, using `_super()` we're able to do that. The next thing we do is bind our new `tabkeydown()` event handler to the `keydown` event.

The `tabkeydown()` handler is a simplified version of the `keydown` event handler provided in the original accordion implementation. If the *Alt* or the *Ctrl* key was pressed in combination with another key, we ignore the event. If the key press was anything other than a *Tab*, we ignore the event too, since we're only interested in altering the *Tab* key behavior when one of the accordion headers is in focus.

The guts of the handler determine what should happen when the *Tab* key is pressed. In which direction should we move the accordion header focus? When do we ignore the event and let the default browser behavior take over? The trick is, figuring out our current index position. If we're on the first header and the user presses *Shift + Tab*, meaning they want to traverse backward, then we don't do anything. Likewise, if we're on the last header and the user presses *Tab*, we pass control back to the browser so as not to interfere with the expected functionality.

Dynamically changing the height style

Accordions are containers that are used to organize and display other UI elements. Thinking about each accordion section as static content is a mistake. The contents of accordion sections do change. For example, a user-triggered event might lead to the creation of a new element within the section. In all likelihood, the components inside a section will change size dynamically, and that's the part we need to be aware of. Why does it matter that accordion contents change size? Since this is an accordion, we'll likely have several sections (or at least a few). Does it make sense to have all of them with a uniform height? It does, until the height of one section grows too large. Then the section heights are no longer uniform. When this happens, we need to take a look at the accordion section height when they change, and potentially adjust some of the height settings on the fly.

Getting ready

Let's use the following markup to create an accordion widget:

```
<div id="accordion">
    <h3>Section 1</h3>
    <div>
        <p>Section 1 content</p>
    </div>
    <h3>Section 2</h3>
    <div>
        <p>Section 2 content</p>
    </div>
    <h3>Section 3</h3>
    <div>
        <p>Section 3 content</p>
    </div>
    <h3>Section 4</h3>
     <div>
        <ul>
            <li>First item</li>
            <li>Second item</li>
            <li>Third item</li>
            <li>Fourth item</li>
        </ul>
    </div>
</div>
```

We'll create the accordion using all the default option values as follows:

```
$(function() {
    $("#accordion").accordion();
});
```

Now, this is where we'll notice a slight inconsistency with regards to height. Here is what the first section looks like. It has minimal content, but uses more space than required.

This is due to the default value of the `heightStyle` option, which says that the height of every section in the accordion will be equal to that of the tallest section. Thus, we have wasted space in the first section. Let's look at the fourth section in the following screenshot to see why this happens:

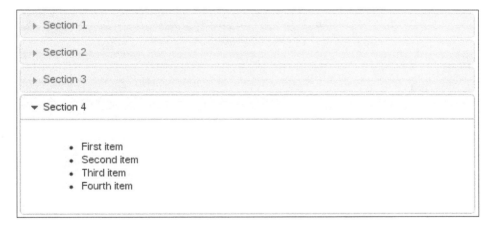

We can see that the first section is as tall as the fourth section. This is due to the `auto` value of `heightStyle`. In this particular example, the difference isn't all that great. That is, the first section doesn't waste too much empty space. Therefore, it would probably make sense to keep this accordion configuration where each section has the same height.

The challenge arises when we're dealing with an application that is dynamically feeding content into a particular accordion section, and at some point where a certain threshold is reached, it no longer makes sense to keep the auto `heightStyle` configuration.

How to do it...

Setting the `heightStyle` to `auto` solves the problem for us, as each section will only use the height necessary to display the content. However, it would be nice if we were able to change this property of the accordion when the height of the content itself changes.

```
(function( $, undefined ) {

$.widget( "ab.accordion", $.ui.accordion, {

    refresh: function() {

        this._super( "refresh" );

        if ( this.options.heightStyle !== "content" ) {
            return;
        }

        this.headers.next().each( function() {

            if ( $( this ).css( "height" ) ) {
                $( this ).css( "height", "" );
            }

        });

    }

});

}) (jQuery);

$(function() {

    $( "#accordion" ).accordion();

    for ( var i=0; i<20; i++ ){
        $( "ul" ).append( "<li>nth item</li>" );
    }

    $( "#accordion" ).accordion( "option", "heightStyle", "content" )
                     .accordion( "refresh" );

});
```

How it works...

What we've done here is extend the accordion widget's `refresh()` method to allow the `heightStyle` option to be changed to content on the fly. The default implementation doesn't allow this. To illustrate this idea, consider the code above where we're creating the accordion widget and adding 20 new items to the last content section. We're using the default section height here, that is, `auto`. So, had we not extended the `refresh()` method to allow this behavior after populating the fourth section, we would have seen a scrollbar here.

Resizable content sections

Resizable content sections allow the user to adjust the height by dragging the bottom of the section. This is a nice alternative having to rely on the `heightStyle` property. Thus, if each section of the accordion can be adjusted by the user, they have the freedom to tailor the accordion layout. For example, if the accordion has a tall section, with wasted space at the bottom, the user might choose to shrink the height of that section to gain a better view of the accordion, and other components of the UI for that matter.

How to do it...

We'll extend the default accordion's `_create()` method by making each content's `div` within the accordion resizable using the resizable interaction widget.

```
( function( $, undefined ) {

$.widget( "ab.accordion", $.ui.accordion, {

    _create: function () {

        this._super( "_create" );

        this.headers.next()
                .resizable( { handles: "s" } )
                .css( "overflow", "hidden" );

    },

    _destroy: function () {

        this._super( "_destroy" );

        this.headers.next()
                .resizable( "destroy" )
```

```
                              .css( "overflow", "" );

        }

    });

    })( jQuery );

    $( function() {

        $( "#accordion" ).accordion();

    });
```

You'll see something similar to the following. Notice that the second section has been dragged down and has the resize mouse cursor.

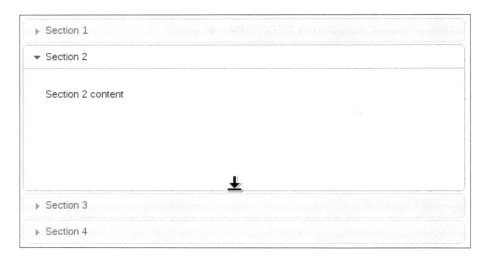

How it works...

Our new version of the _create() method works by first invoking the default accordion's _create() method. Once that completes, we find all content sections of the accordion and apply the resizable() widget. You'll notice, too, that we've told the resizable widget to only show a south handle. This means that the user will only be able to drag any given content section of the accordion up or down, using the cursor at the bottom of the section.

This specialization of an accordion also provides a new implementation of the _delete() method. Once again, we're calling the original accordion's _delete(), after which we're cleaning up the new resizable components we added. This includes removing the overflow CSS property.

There's more...

We can extend our resizable behavior within the accordion by providing a means to turn it off. We'll add a simple `resizable` option to the accordion that checks whether or not to make the accordion sections resizable.

```javascript
(function( $, undefined ) {

$.widget( "ab.accordion", $.ui.accordion, {

    options: {
        resizable: true
    },

    _create: function () {

        this._super( "_create" );

        if ( !this.options.resizable ) {
            return;
        }

        this.headers.next()
                    .resizable( { handles: "s" } )
                    .css( "overflow", "hidden" );
    },

    _destroy: function () {

        this._super( "_destroy" );

        if ( !this.options.resizable ) {
            return;
        }

        this.headers.next()
                    .resizable( "destroy" )
                    .css( "overflow", "" );

    },

});
```

```
})( jQuery );

$(function() {

    $( "#accordion" ).accordion( { resizable: false } );

});
```

Controlling spacing with themes

The space between accordion sections is controlled by the CSS theme framework. In particular, the visual structure for the accordion is defined by a set of CSS rules that can be modified to control the spacing between accordion sections. We could override the accordion theme CSS to adjust for more or less spacing between sections.

How to do it...

We're going to supply an additional CSS module to our UI—one that overrides the accordion structure supplied in the theme we happen to be using. There's no need to fret, however, our change is a simple one. We're going to update the `margin-top` property. In a new CSS file called `theme.accordion.css`, let's add the following style rules:

```
.ui-accordion .ui-accordion-header {
    margin-top: 4px;
}
```

Now that we have the CSS, we need to include it in our HTML header. It should look something like this:

▼ Section 1
Section 1 content
▶ Section 2
▶ Section 3
▶ Section 4

How it works...

We're copying the same CSS selector as is found in any jQuery UI theme. The particular property we've just changed alters the space between the accordion sections. Since we're overriding the default theme value, it's important to include our CSS files after the default theme file. This allows us to override the default theme instead of the default theme overriding our modifications.

Sorting accordion sections

Using the sortable interaction widget, we're able to transform a static accordion section layout into something specified by the user. That is, sortable interaction widgets take a container element, and allow all child elements to be sorted in place. The user does this by dragging the element to the desired order.

We'll look at how we can extend the accordion capabilities so that the sortable section functionality is encapsulated, and can be switched on by a configuration option at the time of creation.

How to do it...

We have to perform several actions when the accordion widget is created, and when the accordion is destroyed. Here is how we extend the widget:

```
( function( $, undefined ) {

$.widget( "ab.accordion", $.ui.accordion, {

    options: {
        sortable: false
    },

    _create: function () {

        this._super( "_create" );

        if ( !this.options.sortable ) {
            return;
        }

        this.headers.each( function() {
            $( this ).next()
                    .addBack()
                    .wrapAll( "<div/>" );
```

```
      });

      this.element.sortable({
          axis: "y",
          handle: "h3",
          stop: function( event, ui ) {
              ui.item.children( "h3" )
                      .triggerHandler( "focusout" );
          }
      });

    },

    _destroy: function () {

      if ( !this.options.sortable ) {
          this._super( "_destroy" );
          return;
      }

      this.element.sortable( "destroy" );

      this.headers.each( function () {
          $( this ).unwrap( "<div/>" );
      });

      this._super( "_destroy" );

    }

  });

})( jQuery );

$( function() {

    $( "#accordion" ).accordion( { sortable: true } );

});
```

With our new accordion widget marked as sortable, users now have the ability to drag header sections around within the accordion. For instance, if the first accordion section belongs to the bottom, the user just drags it to the bottom.

> ▸ Section 2

> ▾ Section 1   🏭

> Section 1 content

> ▸ Section 4

How it works...

With the help of the `sortable()` interaction widget, we're able to extend the default accordion widget implementation to include sorting capabilities. As with any jQuery UI widget enhancements, we don't actually need to extend the widget in question; the new capabilities can always be tacked-on after the widget has been instantiated. However, as you'll see throughout this book, the best practice is to encapsulate customizations and present them to the widget client as a set of options.

Here, we've extended the set of available accordion options to include a `sortable` option. This is how we turn our customization on or off (it is a boolean value). The customized version of `_create()` that we've implemented will call the default version of the accordion's `_create()` method. Afterward, we'll see if the sortable behavior is turned off (in which case we have nothing to do, and so return). Likewise, our custom `_delete()` function checks if the sortable behavior has been turned on after calling the original delete functionality.

The tricky part of implementing sortable accordion sections is the fact that we have to make a slight DOM manipulation inside the accordion element. This is necessary in order to use the sortable interaction widget. Accordion widget markup is structured such that all sections are adjacent to one another. That is, we have an `h3` element, followed by a `div` element. This is one section, and is followed by another `h3` and another `div`, and so on. It is a flat structure. There are two ways to deal with this: alter the markup required to create the widget, or inject some slight DOM modifications, and the widget client is none-the-wiser. We're going the latter route and not requiring the client to change their code. This is another best practice, to keep the existing widget client code functional when providing customizations.

In our customized version of `_create()`, we're iterating over each accordion header and wrapping the header element and the corresponding content element in a `div` element so as to bundle them together. This way, the sortable widget knows how to move this bundle around. Had we not done this, the user would only be able to move the header section, thus severing it from its content. Finally, we're creating the sortable widget, restricting movement to the *y*-axis and setting the movable handle as the accordion header.

Our customized `_destroy()` function undoes our modifications before calling the original `_destroy()` method. This entails unwrapping our new `div` element and destroying the sortable widget.

Dragging-and-dropping between accordions

Some applications require a more fluid layout than others, not just from a screen resolution perspective, but from a functional one too. The accordion widget is a static grouping component that is used to organize smaller components into sections. We can hide all the irrelevant material simply by expanding the section we're interested in. As we have seen in the *Sorting accordion sections* recipe, we can provide an accordion whose structure can be manipulated by the user. Indeed, this has become the expectation of the users en masse—UI configuration by drag-and-drop.

The sortable accordion focuses on a single accordion. In the spirit of giving users freedom within the confines of the application of course, why don't we see if we can support moving an accordion section to a new accordion?

Getting ready

For this experiment, we'll need two basic accordions. The markup should assume a form along the lines of the following:

```
<div id="target-accordion" style="width: 30%">
    <h3>Section 1</h3>
    <div>
        <p>Section 1 content</p>
    </div>
    <h3>Section 2</h3>
    <div>
        <p>Section 2 content</p>
    </div>
    <h3>Section 3</h3>
    <div>
        <p>Section 3 content</p>
    </div>
</div>
<p></p>
<div id="accept-accordion" style="width: 30%">
    <h3>Section 4</h3>
    <div>
        <p>Section 4 content</p>
    </div>
    <h3>Section 5</h3>
```

```
<div>
    <p>Section 5 content</p>
</div>
<h3>Section 6</h3>
<div>
    <p>Section 6 content</p>
</div>
</div>
```

How to do it...

With that in place, let's turn this markup into two accordions. We'll first extend the accordion widget with some fancy drag-and-drop behavior. The intent is to allow the user to drag accordion sections from the first widget to the second. Here is how it's done:

```
(function( $, undefined ) {

$.widget( "ui.accordion", $.ui.accordion, {

    options: {
        target: false,
        accept: false,
        header: "> h3, > div > h3"
    },

    _teardownEvents: function( event ) {

        var self = this,
            events = {};

        if ( !event ) {
            return;
        }

        $.each( event.split(" "), function( index, eventName ) {
            self._off( self.headers, eventName );
        });

    },

    _createTarget: function() {

        var self = this,
            draggableOptions = {
```

```
                handle: "h3",
                helper: "clone",
                connectToSortable: this.options.target,
            };

        this.headers.each( function() {
            $( this ).next()
                        .addBack()
                        .wrapAll( "<div/>" )
                        .parent()
                        .draggable( draggableOptions );
        });
    },

    _createAccept: function() {

        var self = this,
            options = self.options,
            target = $( options.accept ).data( "uiAccordion" );

        var sortableOptions = {

            stop: function ( event, ui ) {

                var dropped        = $(ui.item),
                    droppedHeader = dropped.find("> h3"),
                    droppedClass  = "ui-draggable",
                    droppedId;

                if ( !dropped.hasClass( droppedClass ) ) {
                    return;
                }

                // Get the original section ID, reset the cloned ID.
                droppedId = droppedHeader.attr( "id" );
                droppedHeader.attr( "id", "" );

                // Include dropped item in headers
                self.headers = self.element.find( options.header )

                // Remove old event handlers
                self._off( self.headers, "keydown" );
                self._off( self.headers.next(), "keydown" );
                self._teardownEvents( options.event );
```

```
                // Setup new event handlers, including dropped item.
                self._hoverable( droppedHeader );
                self._focusable( droppedHeader );
                self._on( self.headers, { keydown: "_keydown" } );
                self._on( self.headers.next(), { keydown: "_
panelKeyDown" } );
                self._setupEvents( options.event );


                // Perform cleanup
                $( "#" + droppedId ).parent().fadeOut( "slow",
function() {
                    $( this ).remove();
                    target.refresh();
                });

                dropped.removeClass( droppedClass );

            }

        };

        this.headers.each( function() {
            $(this).next()
                    .addBack()
                    .wrapAll( "<div/>" );
        });

        this.element.sortable( sortableOptions );

    },

    _create: function() {

        this._super( "_create" );

        if ( this.options.target ) {
            this._createTarget();
        }

        if ( this.options.accept ) {
            this._createAccept();
        }
```

```
        },

        _destroy: function() {

            this._super( "_destroy" );

            if ( this.options.target || this.options.accept ) {

                this.headers.each( function() {
                    $( this ).next()
                            .addBack()
                            .unwrap( "<div/>" );
                });
            }
        }

    });

})( jQuery );

$(function() {

    $( "#target-accordion" ).accordion({
        target: "#accept-accordion"
    });

    $( "#accept-accordion" ).accordion({
        accept: "#target-accordion"
    });

});
```

We now have two basic-looking accordion widgets. However, if the user is so inclined, they can drag a section of the first accordion into the second.

How it works...

This might seem like a lot of code at the first glance, but for relatively little (approximately 130 lines), we're able to drag accordion sections out of one accordion and into another. Let's break this down further.

We're adding two accordion options with this widget extension: `target` and `accept`. Target allows us to specify the destination of sections of this accordion. In the example, we used the second accordion as the target for the first accordion, meaning that we can drag from `target-accordion` and drop into `accept-accordion`. But, in order to make that happen, the second accordion needs to be told where to accept sections from; in this case, it is `target-accordion`. We're essentially using these two options to establish a drag-and-drop contract between the two widgets.

This example uses two interaction widgets: draggable and sortable. `target-accordion` uses draggable. If the `target` option was specified, the `_createTarget()` method gets called. The `_createTarget()` method goes through the accordion sections, wraps them in a `div` element, and creates a `draggable()` widget. This is how we're able to drag sections out of the first accordion.

If the `accept` option was specified, the `_createAccept()` method gets called. This follows the same pattern of wrapping each accordion header with its content in a `div` element. Except here, we're making the entire accordion widget `sortable()`.

This may seem counterintuitive. Why would we make the second accordion that wants to accept new sections into sortable? Would it not make more sense to use droppable? We could go down that route, but it would involve a lot of work where we're utilizing the `connectToSortable` option instead. This is a `draggable` option specified in `_createTarget()` where we say that we would like to drop these draggable items into a sortable widget. In this example, sortable is the second accordion.

This solves the problem of deciding on where exactly to drop the accordion section relative to other sections (the sortable widget knows how to handle that). However, an interesting constraint with this approach is that we must clone the dragged item. That is, the section that ultimately gets dropped into the new accordion is just a clone, not the original. So we must deal with that at drop time.

As part of the sortable options defined in `_createAccept()`, we provide a `stop` callback. This callback function is fired when we've dropped a new accordion section into the accordion. Actually, this gets fired for any sorting activity, including new sections being dropped. So, we must take care to check what we're actually working with. We do so by checking whether the item has a `draggable` class attached to it, and if so, we can assume we're dealing with a new accordion section.

Keep in mind that this newly dropped accordion section is simply a clone of the original, so some interesting things need to happen before we can start inserting it into the accordion. First, this new section has the same ID as the original. Eventually, we're going to remove the original from the first accordion, so we store that ID for later use. Once we have it, we can get rid of the dropped section's ID so as to avoid duplicates.

With that taken care of, we have the new DOM element in place, but the accordion widget knows nothing about it. This is where we reload the headers, including the newly-dropped header. The new accordion section still isn't functional because it doesn't handle events properly, so expanding the new section will not work, for example. To avoid strange behavior, we turn off all event handlers and rebind them. This puts the new accordion in its new context while the events are turned on.

We now have a new section in `accept-accordion`. But we can't forget about the original section. It still needs to be removed. Recall that we stored the original section's DOM ID, and we can now safely remove that section and refresh the accordion to adjust the height.

2
Including Autocompletes

In this chapter, we will cover:

- ▶ Styling the default input with themes
- ▶ Building data sources using select options
- ▶ Using multiple data sources
- ▶ Remote autocomplete filtering
- ▶ Custom data and categories
- ▶ Applying effects to the drop-down menu

Introduction

The main purpose of the **autocomplete** widget is to augment the capabilities of the standard HTML form `input` element. Instead of the user having to type out the full value of the input field each time, the autocomplete widget offers suggestions as to what the value might be. For example, let's say you're adding a new product. The product field could be a text input, a select input, and so on. In this scenario, one would use the existing product in the system as the source for an autocomplete widget. Chances are, the user who is entering the product, or another user for that matter, has entered that product before. With autocompletes, users have some assurance that they're providing valid inputs.

Styling the default input with themes

The default autocomplete implementation doesn't change anything visual about the input element. Functionally speaking, we don't want the input element changed. All we need is the drop-down component once the user starts typing. But let's see if we can go ahead and change the virtual appearance of the autocomplete input element using components from the widget framework and the theme framework.

Getting ready

We'll use the following markup for our example, a simple `label` element and a simple `input` element:

```
<div>
    <label for="autocomplete">Items: </label>
    <input id="autocomplete"/>
</div>
```

How to do it...

We'll use the following code to extend the autocomplete widget with the CSS classes from the theme framework we'd like applied. We're introducing a minor behavioral tweak with regards to focus events.

```
( function( $, undefined ) {

$.widget( "ab.autocomplete", $.ui.autocomplete, {

    inputClasses: "ui-widget ui-widget-content ui-corner-all",

    _create: function() {

        this._super( "_create" );
        this._focusable( this.element );
        this.element.addClass( this.inputClasses );

    },

    _destroy: function() {

        this._super( "_destroy" );
        this.element.removeClass( this.inputClasses );
```

```
        }

    });

    }) ( jQuery );

    $( function() {

        var source = [
            'First Item',
            'Second Item',
            'Third Item',
            'Fourth Item'
        ];

        $( "#autocomplete" ).autocomplete( { source: source } );

    });
```

The last thing we need to complete the stylization of our autocomplete's `input` element is a new CSS stylesheet with a couple of rules. The stylesheet should be included in the main HTML where the input markup is defined.

```
input.ui-autocomplete-input {
    padding: 2px;
}

input.ui-autocomplete-input:focus {
    outline: none;
}
```

Here is what our newly-styled autocomplete widget looks like without focus.

Items:

Here is what the autocomplete looks like when it has the focus, and with the drop-down menu expanded.

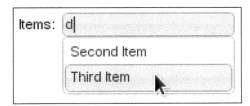

How it works...

When the document loads, we're creating a simple autocomplete using the `#autocomplete` input element.

The first thing you'll notice is the `inputClasses` attribute. This string represents the three classes from the theme framework we want to apply to the widget: `ui-widget`, `ui-widget-content`, and `ui-corner-all`. The `ui-widget` class doesn't do much aside from handling fonts, it's good practice to apply this class to themed elements. The `ui-widget-content` class fixes the input's border for us while the `ui-corner-all` class applies nice rounded corners for us. The reason we've defined this string as an attribute of the widget is because there are two places these classes are used, and this makes for easy maintenance.

The `_create()` method we're overriding here just calls the original implementation of the autocomplete's `_create()` method. Once this completes, we're making the `input` element focusable by calling `_focusable()`. This is a handy utility method defined by the widget factory and inherited by all widgets. It takes care of making the element focusable by applying the `ui-state-focus` CSS class from the theme framework when the element is focused. It also removes the class when the element loses focus. Perhaps, the best part about `_focusable()` is that the widget factory machinery will clean up any focus event handlers for us when the widget is destroyed. The last job of our customized implementation of `_create()` is to add the CSS classes from `inputClasses` to the input element.

As always, we need to make sure we clean up after ourselves when we're finished borrowing from the autocomplete widget. This means extending `_delete()` to ensure that the `inputClasses` attributes are removed from the input element.

Our miniscule CSS rules that we've used to extend the theme framework do two things. The first change is to add a little padding to the `input` element—this is purely aesthetic since the other changes we've made make the text look a little tight inside the input. The second change removes the outline that surrounds the `input` element when focused. This only applies to certain browsers, like Chrome, where an automatic outline is applied.

 Normally, removing the outline isn't advised since accessibility is at stake. But, our changes have taken the focused input into account, so this is fine.

Building data sources using select options

Sometimes, using an array as the source of data for autocomplete widgets isn't the best option. For example, if we already have a `select` element in our user interface, it would make sense to reuse the options in that element to make an autocomplete. Otherwise, we would have to not only design some new code to build the array data source, but we would also have to remove the existing `select` element.

Getting ready

Let's put together some basic markup for this example. Typically, the autocomplete widget expects an `input` as its element. Instead, we're going to give it a `select` element with some simple options.

```
<div>
    <label for="autocomplete">Items: </label>
    <select id="autocomplete">
        <option>First Item</option>
        <option>Second Item</option>
        <option>Third Item</option>
        <option>Fourth Item</option>
    </select>
</div>
```

How to do it...

We'll go ahead and extend the capabilities of the autocomplete widget so that it knows how to handle the `select` elements. After which, we're able to target our `select` element with the autocomplete widget.

```
( function( $, undefined ) {

$.widget( "ab.autocomplete", $.ui.autocomplete, {

    inputClasses: "ui-widget ui-widget-content ui-corner-all",

    _create: function() {

        if ( this.element.is( "select" ) ) {

            var self = this;
            this.original = this.element.hide();
            this.element = $( "<input/>" ).insertAfter( this.original );

            this.options.source = function( request, response ) {

                var filter = $.ui.autocomplete.filter,
                    options = self.original.find( "option" ),
                    result = options.map( function() {
                        return $( this ).val();
```

```
            });

          response( filter( result, request.term ) );

        };

      }

      this._super( "_create" );

    },

    _destroy: function() {

      this._super( "_destroy" );
      this.element.remove();
      this.original.show();

    }

  });

})( jQuery );

$( function() {
    $( "#autocomplete" ).autocomplete();
});
```

Now you should see something that looks like a plain old autocomplete—no `select` element in sight. Further, if you try using the autocomplete, you'll see that the options presented are the same as those in the `select` element's options.

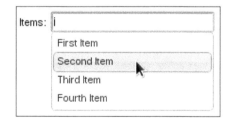

How it works...

Here, we need to add support to the autocomplete widget for `select` elements; we do this at the beginning of our custom `_create()` implementation. If we're dealing with a `select` element, the first thing we do is hide it and store a reference to it in the `original` attribute. Remember, we're only interested in the data source the `select` element has to offer by means of its `options`—we don't want to actually display the `select`. Instead, we're replacing the `select` with an `input` element since this is how the user types and the widget completes.

The `source` option of the autocomplete widget is how we're able to specify a custom function that returns the source data to be used. In our case, we're providing a function that grabs the values from each select `option`. Recall that the `select` element was stored in the `original` attribute earlier. We're using the jQuery `map()` utility function here to turn the `select` options into an array that autocomplete can use. The `filter()` function gets applied, and the `response()` function is sent to the drop-down menu.

When the widget is destroyed, we'd like to restore the original `select` element, since this is what we replaced. The original element gets displayed once again in our customized implementation of `_delete()`—this happens after calling the original `_delete()` method to perform routine cleanup tasks. The `input` element we created is also destroyed here.

Using multiple data sources

Sometimes, an autocomplete widget doesn't map directly to one data source. Take video for instance. Imagine the user needs to pick a video, but the two data sources are DVD and Blu-ray. If we were to use autocomplete to select a video, we would need a way to assign multiple data sources. Furthermore, the mechanism would need to be extensible enough to support adding more data sources, especially since there is a new video format born every other year.

How to do it...

The default implementation of the autocomplete widget is expecting a single data source – an array or an API endpoint string. We'll give the widget a new `sources` option to allow for this behavior. This is how we'll extend autocomplete and create an instance of the widget that has two video data sources – one for DVDs, and one for Blu-ray discs.

```
( function( $, undefined ) {

$.widget( "ab.autocomplete", $.ui.autocomplete, {

    options: {
        sources: []
    },

    _create: function() {

        var sources = this.options.sources;

        if ( sources.length ) {

            this.options.source = function ( request, response ) {

                var merged = [],
```

```
                    filter = $.ui.autocomplete.filter;

            $.each( sources, function ( index, value ) {
                $.merge( merged, value );
            });

            response( filter( merged, request.term ) );

        };

    }

    this._super( "_create" );

},

_destroy: function() {
    this._super( "_destroy" );
}

});

})( jQuery );

$( function() {
    var s1 = [
            "DVD 1",
            "DVD 2",
            "DVD 3"
        ],
        s2 = [
            "Blu-ray 1",
            "Blu-ray 2",
            "Blu-ray 3"
        ];

    $( "#autocomplete" ).autocomplete({
        sources: [s1, s2]
    });
});
```

```
Video: 1
       DVD 1
       Blu-ray 1
```

As you can see, if you were to start searching for the video 1, you'd get versions from each data source in the drop-down menu.

How it works...

Rather than merging our two data sources into one before it gets passed to the autocomplete, we're extending the capabilities of the widget to handle that task for us. In particular, we've added a new `sources` option that can accept several arrays. In the example, we're passing both the DVD and the Blu-ray sources to our widget.

Our customized version of `_create()` checks to see if multiple sources have been supplied by checking the length of the `sources` option. If there are multiple data sources, we use the `merge()` jQuery utility function to create a new array and apply the `filter()` function to it. A good feature of this approach is that it doesn't care how many data sources there are—we could pass a few more to our implementation down the road should the application require it. The merging of these data sources is encapsulated behind the widget.

Remote autocomplete filtering

The autocomplete filtering capabilities aren't just limited to the default implementation, which searches for objects in array sources. We can specify a custom `source()` function that will retrieve only data the user is looking for. This is the ideal approach if you're looking to use autocomplete on a data source with thousands of items. Otherwise, filtering gets too demanding on the browser—the large data set to download, followed by a large array search with each keystroke.

How to do it...

We'll use the GitHub API as the data source for our autocomplete widget. This is a good example since it is much too large to use in the browser memory.

```
$( function() {
  $( "#autocomplete" ).autocomplete({
      minLength: 3,
      source: function( request, response ) {
          $.ajax({
              url: "https://api.github.com/legacy/repos/search/:" +
request.term,
              dataType: "jsonp",
              success: function( resp ) {
                  var repositories = resp.data.repositories.splice(
0, 10 );
                  var items = $.map( repositories, function ( item )
{
```

```
                    return {
                        label: item.name + " (" +
                                item.language + ")",
                        value: item.name
                    };
                });
                response( items );
            }
        });
    }
    });
});
```

Now if you look at the resulting widget in the browser and start typing, you'll see Github repository data in the drop-down menu.

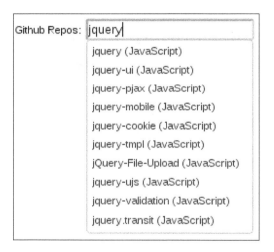

How it works...

Since we're using a large data source, we're telling this particular autocomplete widget that the search for items should only be performed if there are at least three characters. This is done using the `minLength` option. Otherwise, we would be asking the server to query based on one or two characters which isn't what we're after.

The `source` option in our example specifies the data source that we're going to use – the Github API. The function we've passed to the source performs an `$.ajax()` call against the Github API. We're using `jsonp` as the format, which simply means that a callback function from the API will be sent back. We're also passing some query data to the API.

Our success callback function is executed once the API responds with data. We then pass this data through the $.map() utility function in order to produce an array the autocomplete widget understands. Our success function does a simple $.map() on the data to transform it into an array of objects that the autocomplete can use.

There's more...

We can further cut back on the cost of network communication overheads by introducing a term cache to the widget. A **term cache**, as the name suggests, would store locally the results of performing a remote filter operation. This way, when the user inevitably does the exact same thing with their keystrokes, we're not performing the exact same task with the remote API call since we've already cached the result in the widget.

```
( function( $, undefined ) {

$.widget( "ab.autocomplete", $.ui.autocomplete, {

    _cache: {},

    _search: function( value ) {

        var response = this._response(),
            cache = this._cache;

        this.pending++;
        this.element.addClass( "ui-autocomplete-loading" );
        this.cancelSearch = false;

        if ( value in cache ) {
            response( cache[value] );
        }
        else {
            this.source( { term: value }, response );
        }

    }

});

})( jQuery );

$( function() {
    $( "#autocomplete" ).autocomplete({
        minLength: 3,
        source: function( request, response ) {
```

```
              var self = this;
              $.ajax({
                  url: "https://api.github.com/legacy/repos/search/:" +
      request.term,

                  dataType: "jsonp",
                  success: function( resp ) {
                      var repositories = resp.data.repositories.splice(
      0, 10 );

                      var items = $.map( repositories, function ( item )
      {

                          return {
                              label: item.name + " (" +
                                      item.language + ")",
                              value: item.name
                          };
                      });
                      self._cache[request.term] = items;
                      response( items );
                  }
              });
          }
      });
  });
```

You can see where we've made changes in the preceding code to support caching the items returned from the HTTP request. Now we're extending the widget to add the new `_cache` attribute. We're also extending the `_search()` function, which is in charge of checking for a cached value. If it finds one, the rendering response is called using the cached version of the data. The `source()` function is responsible for storing cached results, but this is a simple one-liner.

Custom data and categories

One approach to separating two categories of autocomplete data might be to have two distinct fields, each with their own autocomplete widgets. Another would be to introduce the notion of a category into the widget itself. When the drop-down menu appears to suggest items for the user, they will also see the category the item belongs to. To do this in the autocomplete widget, we need to change both how the widget understands the source data, and how the menu items are rendered.

How to do it...

We're going to extend the autocomplete widget in order to change how the menu items are rendered. We also need to consider the data passed into the widget as the source.

```
( function( $, undefined ) {

$.widget( "ab.autocomplete", $.ui.autocomplete, {

    _renderMenu: function( ul, items ) {

        var that = this,
            currentCategory = "";

        items.sort(function( a, b ) {
            return a.cat > b.cat
        });

        $.each( items, function( index, item ) {

            if ( item.cat != currentCategory ) {
                that._renderCategory( ul, item );
                currentCategory = item.cat;
            }

            that._renderItemData( ul, item );

        });

    },

    _renderCategory: function( ul, item ) {
        return $( "<li>" ).addClass( "ui-autocomplete-category" )
                        .html( item.cat )
                        .appendTo( ul );
    },

    _renderItem: function( ul, item ) {
        return $( "<li>" ).addClass( "ui-autocomplete-item" )
                        .append( $( "<a>" )
                        .append( $( "<span>" ).html( item.label ) )
                        .append( $( "<span>" ).html( item.desc ) ) )
```

```
                                    .appendTo( ul );
        }

    });

    })( jQuery );

    $( function() {

        var items = [
            {
                value: "First Item",
                label: "First Item",
                desc: "A description of the first item goes here",
                cat: "Completed"
            },
            {
                value: "Second Item",
                label: "Second Item",
                desc: "A description of the second item goes here",
                cat: "In Progress"
            },
            {
                value: "Third Item",
                label: "Third Item",
                desc: "A description of the third item goes here",
                cat: "Completed"
            }
        ];

        $( "#autocomplete" ).autocomplete( {source: items} );

    });
```

We're almost done. The changes we've made to the menu will not just magically work out, we need to apply some styles. The following CSS code should be included on the page:

```
.ui-autocomplete-category {
    font-weight: bold;
    padding: .2em .4em;
    margin: .8em 0 .2em;
    line-height: 1.5;
}

.ui-autocomplete-item > a > span {
    display: block;
}
```

```
.ui-autocomplete-item > a > span + span {
    font-size: .9em;
}
```

Now, if you start typing in the autocomplete, you'll notice a drop-down menu drastically different from what we're used to as it contains both category and description information.

How it works...

The goal of this widget extension is to accept custom source data and to use that data in the display of the drop-down menu. Specifically, the new data we're working with is the category and the description. The category is a one-to-many relationship with the items insofar, as several items we pass to the widget may have the same category string. Our job is to figure out which items fall under any given category and to represent this structure in the drop-down menu. Additionally, the description of the item is a one-to-one relationship, so less work is required here but we nonetheless would like to include the description in the drop-down menu.

The first method from the original implementation that we're overriding is `_renderMenu()`. The job of `_renderMenu()` is to alter the underlying HTML structure each time a suggestion is made to the user. We keep track of the current category with `currentCategory`. We then render each item with `_renderItem()`.

The `_renderCategory()` function renders the category text as an `<li>`. It also adds the `ui-autocomplete-category` class. Likewise, our `_renderItem()` function renders the item text, and it is here that we also make use of the `desc` attribute. The item also has the `ui-autocomplete-item` class.

The new CSS styles we've included in our UI are a necessary component of the new version of autocomplete that we've created. Without them, the description would be of the same font size and would display on the same line as the item label. Likewise, the category needs the newly-added styles to stand out as a category that groups other items instead of just another item.

There's more...

Whenever we extend the data used by the autocomplete widget, we have to tell the widget how to work with it. Here, we've told autocomplete how to display the new data in the drop-down menu. Alternatively, we could tell the widget to perform filtering on some data fields that the user never actually sees in the drop down-menu. Or we could combine the two.

Here is how we would go about using both the category and the description, both non-standard fields, in the filtering when the user starts typing.

```
$.ui.autocomplete.filter = function( array, term ) {

    var matcher = new RegExp( $.ui.autocomplete.escapeRegex( term ),
"i" );

    return $.grep( array, function( value ) {
        return matcher.test( value.cat ) ||
            matcher.test( value.desc ) ||
            matcher.test( value.label )
    });

};
```

Here we're replacing the `filter()` function that autocomplete uses with our own implementation. The two are similar, we're just adapting the `RegExp.test()` calls to the `desc` and `cat` field. We would place this code just beneath the custom widget declaration of autocomplete. The reason this is done externally to the customization specification is because `autocomplete.filter()` is kind of like a static method. Where with other methods, we're overriding on a per-instance basis.

Applying effects to the drop-down menu

By default, we get a fairly simplistic presentation of the drop-down menu containing suggestions for completion based on what we type. The menu is simply displayed, without much fuss. Which is fine, it gets the job done reliably. But, on the other hand, there is always something we can do to make the UI look more polished. It could be as simple as changing the autocomplete widget in your application to use some subtle effects while transitioning to a visible state.

Getting ready

Since what we're after here is really more of a visual presentation aspect of the widget, we're probably safe using any existing instance of the widget.

How to do it...

Let's build on the default implementation of the autocomplete widget to include some subtle animations for the drop-down menu.

```
( function( $, undefined ) {

$.widget( "ab.autocomplete", $.ui.autocomplete, {

    _suggest: function( items ) {

        this._resetMenu();
        this._renderMenu( this.menu.element, items );
        this.menu.refresh();

        this._resizeMenu();
        this._positionMenu();

    },

    _resetMenu: function() {

        this.menu.element
                .empty()
                .zIndex( this.element.zIndex() + 1 );

    },

    _positionMenu: function() {

        var pos = $.extend( { of: this.element }, this.options.
position );
        this.menu.element.position( pos );

    },

    _resizeMenu: function() {

        var menu = this.menu,
            exclude = 0;
            target = Math.max(
                menu.element.width( "" ).outerWidth() + 1,
                this.element.outerWidth()
            ),
            excludeCSS = [
```

```
                    'borderLeftWidth',
                    'borderRightWidth',
                    'paddingLeft',
                    'paddingRight'
              ];

        if( menu.element.is( ":hidden" ) ) {
            menu.element.css( { display: "block", opacity: 0 } );
        }

        $.each( excludeCSS , function( index, item ) {
            exclude += parseFloat( menu.element.css( item ) );
        });

        if ( menu.element.css( "opacity" ) == 0 ) {
            menu.element.animate({
                width: target - exclude,
                opacity: 1
            }, 300);
        }
        else{
            menu.element.width( target - exclude );
        }

    },

    _close: function( event ) {

        var menu = this.menu;

        if ( menu.element.is( ":visible" ) ) {

            menu.element.fadeOut();
            menu.blur();
            this.isNewMenu = true;
            this._trigger( "close", event );

        }

    }

});

})( jQuery );
```

```
$(function() {
    var source = [
        "First Item",
        "Second Item",
        "Third Item",
        "Fourth Item"
    ];
    $( "#autocomplete" ).autocomplete({
        source: source,
    });
});
```

If you start using this autocomplete widget by typing in the input element, you'll notice that the drop-down menu glides smoothly into view instead of just popping out abruptly. Also, when the menu is no longer needed, it fades out of existence.

How it works...

The autocomplete is being extended here so we can inject our customized animation functionality. But this time around, the changes are a little more involved, we're not merely extending _create() with a few lines of code. There are a few methods buried deep in the autocomplete code that we need to extend. We've also introduced a few new methods of our own in the autocomplete widget.

The first method we're overriding is _suggest(). The _suggest() method is called by the autocomplete widget when the user has typed the minimum length of characters to perform a search. The original method takes care of everything that needs to happen in terms of rendering and displaying the drop-down menu. In our version of the method, we're just calling other methods of the widget. The job of _suggest() is to orchestrate everything that takes place when a search happens. There are two logical steps taken here. First, the menu is rendered with the new content. Next, the menu is displayed, resized, and positioned. The latter is where the animation takes place.

We won't drill into the details of the _resetMenu() and _positionMenu() methods as those code snippets are taken from the original implementation for the most part. They just empty and position the menu, respectively.

The _resizeMenu() method is where the actual animation takes place when the menu is displayed. This is a longer method because we have to perform a few calculations to pass into animate(). The original implementation of _resizeMenu() uses the outerWidth() jQuery function to set the width of the menu. This is to get proper alignment with the input element. However, we want to animate the width change. So we must manually compute the inner width. The outer width values go in the exclude variable. The inner width is target - exclude.

We check if the menu is already displayed before actually showing it, and before animating it. If the element isn't visible, we change the `display` CSS property, but set the `opacity` property to `0`. The reason we do this is that we need the element's box model dimensions in order to position it. But, we still haven't applied the animation effects to the menu. Here, we check if the `opacity` property for the menu is at `0`. If not, that means the menu is already displayed and it would not make sense to re-animate it now. Otherwise, we execute the width and opacity animation.

Finally, the `_close()` method replaces the original autocomplete `_close()` implementation. The code is nearly the same as the original, except we do a basic `fadeOut()` when the menu is closed, as opposed to merely hiding it.

This extension of the autocomplete does not implement an option that will turn off this behavior. This is alright because the extension only does one thing—apply effects to the drop-down menu. So, to disable these effects, we can just disable extension. The extension of a widget is defined inside a function that calls itself. When the script first loads, the function is called, and the widget gets extended with the new behavior. We can disable the behavior part of the function that invokes itself.

```
(function( $, undefined ) {
    // Code that extends a jQuery UI widget...
}); //( jQuery );
```

3
Crafting Buttons

In this chapter, we will cover:

- ▶ Making simple checklists
- ▶ Controlling the spacing within buttonsets
- ▶ Filling space with buttons automatically
- ▶ Sorting buttons within a group
- ▶ Using effects with the button hover state
- ▶ Button icons and hiding text

Introduction

The **button** widget is an easy way to decorate the HTML button and link elements in your user interface. With a simple call to the button widget, we're able to decorate the standard elements with the theme framework found in jQuery UI. Additionally, there are two types of buttons. There is the singular notion of a button, the more popular use case. But there is also the notion of a **buttonset**—used in cases where we would like to decorate checkboxes and radio buttons found in typical HTML forms.

In this chapter, we take a much closer look at what the button entails, covering some usage scenarios by example. We'll go from the simple usage, such as creating a checklist and sorting buttons, to more advanced usage, such as applying effects and automatically filling space. Along the way, you'll learn how the widget framework supports developers in extending the button where it doesn't quite do what they need it to.

Making simple checklists

Checklists are easy enough to do in plain old HTML, all you really need are some checkboxes and some labels beside them. If you're using a widget framework such as jQuery UI, however, we can enhance that list with ease. The button widget knows how to behave when applied to an `input` element of type `checkbox`. So let's start off with a basic list and see how we can apply the button widget to the `input` elements. We'll also see if we can take the user interactivity a step further with some state and icon enhancements.

Getting ready

Let's start by creating a simple HTML `div` to hold our checklist. Inside, each item is represented by an `input` element of type `checkbox`, along with a `label` for the element.

```
<div>
    <input type="checkbox" id="first" />
    <label for="first">Item 1</label>
    <input type="checkbox" id="second" />
    <label for="second">Item 2</label>
    <input type="checkbox" id="third" />
    <label for="third">Item 3</label>
    <input type="checkbox" id="fourth" />
    <label for="fourth">Item 4</label>
</div>
```

With this markup, we actually have a functioning checklist UI, albeit, a less-than-usable one. We can use the toggling capability of the jQuery UI button widget to encapsulate the `label` and the `checkbox` together as a checklist item.

How to do it...

We'll introduce the following JavaScript code to collect our `checkbox` inputs and use their `labels` to assemble the **toggle button** widget.

```
$(function() {

    $( "input" ).button( { icons: { primary: "ui-icon-bullet" } } );

    $( "input" ).change( function( e ) {

        var button = $( this );

        if ( button.is( ":checked" ) ) {
```

```
        button.button( "option", {
            icons: { primary: "ui-icon-check" }
        });

    }
    else {

        button.button( "option", {
            icons: { primary: "ui-icon-bullet" }
        });

    }

    });

});
```

With that, you have a toggle-button checklist, complete with icons to assist in conveying the state. When the user clicks on the toggle-button, it goes into "on" state, which is depicted by the change in background color, and other theme properties. We've also added icons that toggle along with the button state.

How it works...

Our event handler, fired when the DOM is ready, requires only one line of code to turn the `input` elements on the page into toggle buttons. Within the button constructor, we're specifying that the default icon to use is the `ui-icon-bullet` icon class from the theme framework. The button widget knows that we're creating a toggle button because of the underlying HTML element. Since these are checkboxes, the widget will change its behavior when the button is clicked—in the case of a `checkbox`, we want the button to give the appearance of toggling on and off. Additionally, the button widget knows which `label` belongs to which button based on the `for` attribute. For example, the label for `for="first"` will be assigned to the button with `id="first"`.

Next we apply the `change` event handler to all our buttons. This handler is the same for each button, so we can bind it to all buttons at once. The job of this handler is to update the button icon. We don't have to change anything else about the button state because the default button implementation will do that for us. All we need to do in our event handler is check the state on the `checkbox` itself. If checked, we show the `ui-icon-check` icon. Otherwise, we show the `ui-icon-bullet` icon.

Controlling the spacing with buttonsets

The jQuery UI toolkit gives developers a container widget used for working with groups of buttons called a **buttonset**. You would use a buttonset for things like groups of checkboxes or groups of radio buttons—things that form a collaborative set.

The default appearance of the buttonset is of a unified whole. That is, the goal is to form a seemingly single widget out of several buttons. By default, the buttonset widget has no spacing controls for the developer. The buttons within the set, by default, are all stacked up against one another. This may not be what we're after, depending on the context of the buttonset widget in our overall user interface.

Getting ready

To better illustrate the spacing constraints we're presented with, let's build a buttonset widget and look at the result before we go about trying to resolve the issue. We'll use the following group of radio buttons as our markup:

```
<div>
    <input type="radio" id="first" name="items" />
    <label for="first">Item 1</label>
    <input type="radio" id="second" name="items" />
    <label for="second">Item 2</label>
    <input type="radio" id="third" name="items" />
    <label for="third">Item 3</label>
    <input type="radio" id="fourth" name="items"/>
    <label for="fourth">Item 4</label>
</div>
```

And we'll create the buttonset widget as follows:

```
$(function() {
    $( "div" ).buttonset();
});
```

Here is what our buttonset looks like. Notice that this widget still exhibits radio button functionality. Here the third item is selected, but will become deselected if I were to click elsewhere in the widget.

How to do it...

Now, there is nothing wrong with the default presentation of the buttonset widget. The only potential challenge we might face is if we have a spacing theme happening elsewhere in the application—the stacked against one another look of the widget just might not fit in from an aesthetic perspective. We can tackle this issue with relatively little effort by extending the widget with an option that allows us to "explode" the buttons so that they're no longer touching.

We'll implement this new exploding `buttonset` capability by extending the buttonset widget and adding a new option that will enable this behavior. The HTML stays the same as previous, but here is the new JavaScript code.

```
(function( $, undefined ) {

$.widget( "ab.buttonset", $.ui.buttonset, {

    options: {
        exploded: false
    },

    refresh: function() {

        this._super("refresh");

        if ( !this.options.exploded ) {
            return;
        }

        var buttons = this.buttons.map(function() {
            return $( this ).button( "widget" )[ 0 ];
        });

        this.element.addClass( "ui-buttonset-exploded" );
```

```
            buttons.removeClass( "ui-corner-left ui-corner-right" )
                .addClass( "ui-corner-all" );

    }

});

})( jQuery );

$(function() {
    $( "div" ).buttonset( { exploded: true } );
});
```

We'll want to include the following CSS on the page—including it via a new stylesheet is the recommended practice here:

```
.ui-buttonset-exploded .ui-button {
    margin: 1px;
}
```

How it works...

Our extension of the buttonset widget adds the `exploded` option, allowing the programmer using the widget to specify whether they would like the individual buttons separated from one another or not. We also override the `refresh()` method here in order to alter the display if the `exploded` option is `true`.

To do this, we create a jQuery object representing all the individual buttons in the buttonset. The reason we're using `map()` here is because of a work-around required with `checkbox` and `radio` buttons. The `ui-buttonset-exploded` class adds the `margin` that we're looking for between the buttons—it explodes them outward. Next, we remove the `ui-corner-left` and `ui-corner-right` classes from any of the buttons, and add the `ui-corner-all` class to each button that gives them each their own independent borders.

Filling space with buttons automatically

The width of any given button widget is controlled by what goes inside it. What this amounts to is either the primary or secondary icons, or neither, plus the text. The actual rendered width of the button itself isn't concretely specified, but instead is determined by the browser. Of course, this is a desirable feature of any widget—relying on the browser to compute dimensions. This approach scales well when there are lots of widgets in the UI to consider, and when there are lots of browser resolution configurations to consider.

There are, however, a few cases where the automatic width set forth by the browser isn't desirable. Think about several buttons in the same context, perhaps a `div` element. In all likelihood, these buttons will not render as having the same width, when this is in fact a desired property. Just because one button in the group has slightly more or slightly less text doesn't mean that we don't want them to share a consistent width.

Getting ready

The goal here is to treat the widest button within a group of buttons as the target width. The siblings of the group get notified when a new button is added, potentially creating a new target width if it is the widest. Let's illustrate the problem further by looking at the default button functionality and what it means in terms of width.

Here is the HTML we'll use to create the button widgets.

```
<div>
    <button style="display: block;">Button 1</button>
    <button style="display: block;">Button 2</button>
    <button style="display: block;">Button with longer text</button>
</div>
```

We're explicitly marking each button as a block-level element so we can easily contrast the widths. Notice, too, that the buttons are all siblings.

The following JavaScript turns each button element into a button widget.

```
$(function() {
    $( "button" ).button();
});
```

As you can see, the first two buttons are of the same length while the last button uses more text and is the widest.

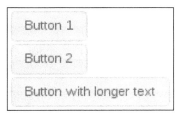

How to do it...

Let's now extend the button widget with some new behavior that allows the developer to synchronize the width of each button within a group. The modified JavaScript code to extend the button widget looks like this:

```
(function( $, undefined ) {

$.widget( "ab.button", $.ui.button, {

    options: {
        matchWidth: false
    },

    _create: function() {

        this._super( "create" );

        if ( !this.options.matchWidth ) {
            return;
        }

        this.element.siblings( ":" + this.widgetFullName )
                .addBack()
                .button( "refresh" );

    },

    refresh: function() {

        this._super( "refresh" );

        if ( !this.options.matchWidth ) {
            return;
        }

        var widths = this.element
                        .siblings( ":" + this.widgetFullName )
                        .addBack()
                        .children( ".ui-button-text" )
                        .map(function() {
                            return $( this ).width();
                        }),
            maxWidth = Math.max.apply( Math, widths ),
            buttonText = this.element.children( ".ui-button-text" );

        if ( buttonText.width() < maxWidth ) {
            buttonText.width( maxWidth );
        }
```

```
        }

    });

    })( jQuery );

    $(function() {
        $( "button" ).button( { matchWidth: true } );
    });
```

Here you can see that the buttons communicate with one another to establish the correct width for each sibling within the group. In other words, the first two buttons altered their widths as a result of the last button being added to the group.

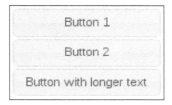

How it works...

The extension to the button widget we've just added creates a new `matchWidth` option, which, if `true`, will change the width of this button to match that of the widest in this group if necessary.

Our extension of the `_create()` method calls the default `_create()` button implementation, and then we tell all our siblings to `refresh()`. We include this button in the list of siblings by using `addBack()`—the reason being, we might have to adjust our own width if there is already someone bigger than us. Alternatively, if we're now the widest sibling, we have to tell everyone so that they can adjust their widths.

The `refresh()` method calls the base `refresh()` implementation, then figures out whether the width of this button should be updated or not. The first step is to generate a width array for all siblings in the group, including ourselves. With an array of widths, we can pass it to `Math.max()` to get the maximum width. If the current width of this button is less than the widest button in the group, we adjust to the new width.

Notice that we're not actually collecting or changing the width of the button element itself, but rather, the `span` element within. This `span` has the `ui-button-text` class, and is the element of variable width we're interested in. If we took the other route of simply measuring the button's width, we could end up with some messy margin issues that leave us in a state worse than we were in to begin with.

There's more...

You'll notice in the previous example that the text of the resized buttons remained centered. We could, if so inclined, introduce a small CSS adjustment when making button width changes that would keep the button text aligned.

```
(function( $, undefined ) {

$.widget( "ab.button", $.ui.button, {

    options: {
        matchWidth: false
    },

    _create: function() {

        this._super( "create" );

        if ( !this.options.matchWidth ) {
            return;
        }

        this.element.siblings( ":" + this.widgetFullName )
                .addBack()
                .button( "refresh" );

    },

    _destroy: function() {
        this._super();
        this.element.css( "text-align", "" );
    },

    refresh: function() {

        this._super( "refresh" );

        if ( !this.options.matchWidth ) {
            return;
        }

        var widths = this.element
```

```
                              .siblings( ":" + this.widgetFullName )
                              .addBack()
                              .children( ".ui-button-text" )
                              .map(function() {
                                  return $( this ).width();
                              }),
                 maxWidth = Math.max.apply( Math, widths ),
                 buttonText = this.element.children( ".ui-button-text" );

             if ( buttonText.width() < maxWidth ) {
                 buttonText.width( maxWidth );
                 this.element.css( "text-align", "left" );
             }

         }

    });

})( jQuery );

$(function() {
    $( "button" ).button( { matchWidth: true } );
});
```

Notice that within the _refresh() method, we're now stating that the text-align CSS property is left. Additionally, we have to add a new _destroy() method to clean up this property when the button is destroyed. The end result is the same as our previous example, except now the button text is aligned.

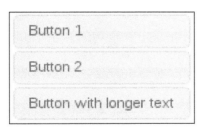

Sorting buttons within a group

We can use the sortable() interaction widget to provide the user which some flexibility. Why not let the user move buttons around? Especially given the small amount of code it takes.

Getting ready

We'll use a list to organize our buttons, as follows:

```
<ul>
    <li><a href="#">Button 1</a></li>
    <li><a href="#">Button 2</a></li>
    <li><a href="#">Button 3</a></li>
</ul>
```

We'll use the following CSS to fix the list layout to better display button widgets.

```
ul {
    list-style-type: none;
    padding: 0;
}

li {
    margin: 4px;
}
```

How to do it...

The JavaScript code to make this happen is actually quite miniscule—we create the buttons, then we apply the sortable interaction widget.

```
$(function() {
    $( "a" ).button();
    $( "ul" ).sortable({
        opacity: 0.6
    });
});
```

At this point, we're able to drag-and-drop buttons—but only within the designated container element, in this case, ul.

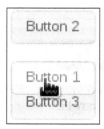

How it works...

The first thing we're doing in this example, once the document is ready, is creating the button widgets. We're using anchors as the underlying element, which works just as well as `button` elements. You'll notice too, that we've structured the button widgets on the page inside of an unordered list. The styles added to the page just remove the list indentation and the bullets. But the `ul` element is what we're targeting for the sortable interaction. By default, the sortable widget looks for all child elements and makes them the sortable items, in our case, these are `li` elements. The `opacity` option specified in the example tells `sortable` to change the visual opacity of the element being dragged.

Using effects with the button hover state

The button widget utilizes the various states found in the jQuery UI theme framework. For example, when the user hovers over a button widget, this event triggers a handler inside the button widget that applies the `ui-state-hover` class to the element, changing its appearance. Likewise, when the mouse leaves the widget, a different handler removes that class.

This default functionality of the button widget works fine—it just uses the `addClass()` and `removeClass()` jQuery functions to apply the hover class. As the user moves around and considers what he/she wants to do next, the mouse is likely to move in and out of button widgets; this is where we tweak the experience by providing the user with some subtle effects.

Getting ready

For this example, we'll just create three simple button elements that will serve as the button widgets. This way, we can experiment with moving the mouse pointer over several buttons.

```
<div>
    <button>Button 1</button>
    <button>Button 2</button>
    <button>Button 3</button>
</div>
```

How to do it...

Let's extend the capabilities of the default button widget to include a new option called `animateHover` that when `true`, animates the addition and removal of the `ui-state-hover` class.

```
(function( $, undefined ) {

$.widget( "ab.button", $.ui.button, {
```

```
        options: {
            animateHover: false
        },

        _create: function() {

            this._super( "create" );

            if ( !this.options.animateHover ) {
                return;
            }

            this._off( this.element, "mouseenter mouseleave" );

            this._on({
                mouseenter: "_mouseenter",
                mouseleave: "_mouseleave"
            });

        },

        _mouseenter: function( e ) {
            this.element.stop( true, true )
                        .addClass( "ui-state-hover", 200 );
        },

        _mouseleave: function( e ) {
            this.element.stop( true, true )
                        .removeClass( "ui-state-hover", 100 );
        }

    });

})( jQuery );

$(function() {
    $( "button" ).button( { animateHover: true } );
});
```

How it works...

We've added a new option to the button widget called animateHover. When true, buttons will animate the addition or removal of the CSS properties found in ui-state-hover class. This is all done by overriding the _create() method, called when the button widget is first instantiated. Here, we're checking if the animateHover option is false, after we call the original _create() method that performs routine button initialization tasks.

If the option is set, the first job is unbinding the original `mouseenter` and `mouseleave` event handlers from the button. These handlers are what, by default, simply add or remove the hover class. This is exactly what we want to change, so once the original handlers are removed, we're free to register our own using `_on()`. This is where we use the `stop()`, `addClass()`, and `removeClass()` functions. The jQuery UI effects extensions apply to the `addClass()` and `removeClass()` functions if a duration is given after the class name, which we've done here. We want the adding of the `ui-state-hover` class to take `200` milliseconds and the removal of the class to take `100` milliseconds since the initial hover is more noticeable by the user. Finally, the `stop( true, true )` call is a common technique in jQuery for ensuring animations don't overlap and cause jittery behavior from the user perspective.

Button icons and hiding text

With buttons, developers can choose to render icon-only buttons. This is accomplished by telling the button we don't want the text displayed. This is easy enough to do and serves a number of use cases—often, depending on context, an icon will suffice in explaining its action. What's more, we can add the button label back any time we wish with a simple option change. We can do this because the button text is part of the underlying HTML component. With icons, however, things become a little trickier because they're an adornment on the button. We can't turn the icons on and off as we can do with the text—the entire icon specification needs to be applied once again.

Something to aim for, then, would be a method to specify the icons in the button constructor, but remember them once turned off. This way, the icons will behave as though they're part of the original DOM element.

Getting ready

We'll start with creating the structure necessary for three icon buttons. We'll also introduce two links that alter the state of each button.

```
<div>
    <button class="play">Play</button>
    <button class="pause">Pause</button>
    <button class="stop">Stop</button>
</div>

<div>
    <br/>
    <a href="#" class="no-icons">no icons</a>
    <br/>
    <a href="#" class="icons">icons</a>
</div>
```

How to do it...

We'll provide the button widget with our icon toggling capability by adding a new `icon` option. The idea, remember, is to provide the same capability as the `text` option, except for icons.

```
(function( $, undefined ) {

$.widget( "ab.button", $.ui.button, {

    options: {
        icon: true
    },

    _hiddenIcons: {},

    _setOption: function( key, value ) {

        if ( key != "icon" ) {
            this._superApply( arguments );
            return;
        }

        if ( !value && !$.isEmptyObject( this.options.icons ) ) {
            this._hiddenIcons = this.options.icons;
            this._super( "text", true );
            this._super( "icons", {} );
        }
        else if ( value && $.isEmptyObject( this.options.icons ) ) {
            this._super( "icons", this._hiddenIcons );
        }

    },

    _create: function() {

        if ( !this.options.icon ) {
            this._hiddenIcons = this.options.icons;
            this.options.icons = {};
        }

        this._superApply( arguments );

    }
```

```
});

})( jQuery );

$(function() {

    $( "a.no-icons" ).click( function( e ) {
        e.preventDefault();
        $( "button" ).button( "option", "icon", false );
    });

    $( "a.icons" ).click( function( e ) {
        e.preventDefault();
        $( "button" ).button( "option", "icon", true );
    });

    $( "button" ).button( {text: false} );

    $( ".play" ).button( "option", {
        icons: { primary: "ui-icon-play" }
    });

    $( ".pause" ).button( "option", {
        icons: { primary: "ui-icon-pause" }
    });

    $( ".stop" ).button( "option", {
        icons: { primary: "ui-icon-stop" }
    });

});
```

How it works...

Initially, the three buttons are created with `text` disabled, even though the button text still exists as part of the underlying DOM element. Next, we set the `icon` option for each of the three buttons. When the page first loads, you should just see icon buttons.

The two links on the page, **no icons** and **icons** remove and add icons to the button widgets, respectively. The function callback for each link does this by setting a value for the custom `icon` option we've added to the `button` widget. Clicking on the **no icons** link would result in the button icons being removed, and replaced with their text.

By clicking on the **icons** link, we're re-enabling the `icons` option we had set previously for each button. This is done by changing our custom `icon` button, so if we click on that link now, we can see that our icons are restored, without having to specify what icons were used.

You'll notice that by setting the `icon` value to `true`, we didn't hide the text, as was the case in the original state of the buttons. We can still do this by manually setting `text` to `false`, but that should be a manual process, and not a modification by our button extension.

Our extension adds a new `_hiddenIcons` attribute where we can store the value of the `icons` option when the `icon` option is set to `false`. We perform the bulk of our work in `_setOption()`, which is called any time a developer wants to set an option on the widget. We only care about the new `icon` option we've added. First, we check if we're disabling the icons, in which case, we store a copy of the `icons` option in the `_hiddenIcons` attribute so that it can be restored at another time. We also set the `text` option to `true`, so that the text will display if hidden. It would be a bad idea to hide the button icon and the text at the same time. Finally, we actually hide the icons by unsetting the `icons` option.

If, on the other hand, we're enabling icons, we need to look them up in the `_hiddenIcons` attribute and set them as the `icons` button option. The `_create()` implementation we're overriding here simply stores the icons setting in `_hiddenIcons` and hides them if this has been specified when the widget is first created.

4
Developing Datepickers

In this chapter, we will cover:

- ▶ Working with different date formats
- ▶ Making a full-sized calendar widget
- ▶ Displaying month-to-month effects
- ▶ Appointment reminders as tooltips
- ▶ Restricting the date range
- ▶ Hiding the input field
- ▶ Additional data and controls

Introduction

The **datepicker** widget augments the typical text input form element by presenting the user with a date selection utility. We see these types of inputs everywhere on the Web now. The graphical nature of the datepicker is intuitive for most users because it closely resembles a physical calendar. The datepicker widget also addresses the challenge of working with consistent date formats, something users don't have to worry about.

Working with different date formats

The datepicker widget supports a variety of date string formats. The date string is the value populated in the text input when the user makes a selection. More often than not, applications will try to follow the same date format throughout the UI for consistency. So if you're not happy with the default format provided by the widget, we can change it when the widget is created using the `dateFormat` option.

How to do it...

We'll start by creating two `input` fields where we require the date input from the user:

```
<div>
    <label for="start">Start:</label>
    <input id="start" type="text" size="30"/>
</div>

<div>
    <label for="stop">Stop:</label>
    <input id="stop" type="text" size="30"/>
</div>
```

Next, we'll create two datepicker widgets using the preceding `input` fields and by specifying our custom format.

```
$(function() {

    $( "input" ).datepicker({
        dateFormat: "DD, MM d, yy"
    });

});
```

How it works...

When we make a selection in either of the datepicker widgets, you'll notice the text `input` value changes to the selected date, using the format we've chosen. The date format string itself, `"DD, MM d, yy"`, is modeled after those found in most other programming languages, that is, there is no native JavaScript date formatting facilities for the datepicker to use. When the user makes a selection in the drop-down calendar of the datepicker, a `Date` object is created. The widget then uses the `dateFormat` option to format the `Date` object, and populate the text input with the result.

There's more...

If we're building a reasonably large user interface, we'll probably use several datepicker widgets in several different places. To keep up with the date formatting consistency, we'll have to specify the `dateFormat` option each time we create the datepicker widget. We will likely have several calls to create the widget that use different selectors, so it becomes a little tedious to always specify the same `dateFormat` option when it should just be the default.

In this scenario, we're better off just changing the default `dateFormat` value to something our application uses throughout. This beats having to specify the same format, over and over, while preserving the ability to change the date format on a case-by-case basis.

We'll use the same HTML structure as before—the two `input` fields are our datepicker placeholders. But let's modify the JavaScript as follows:

```
(function( $, undefined ) {

$.widget( "ui.datepicker", $.ui.datepicker, {
    options: $.extend(
        $.ui.datepicker.prototype.options,
        { dateFormat: "DD, MM d, yy" }
    ),
});

})( jQuery );

$(function() {

    $( "#start" ).datepicker();
    $( "#stop" ).datepicker();

});
```

Now, if you run this modified JavaScript, you'll get the same datepicker behavior as before. What you'll notice, however, is that we're now making two calls to the `datepicker()` constructor. Neither specifies the `dateFormat` option, because we've altered the default value by customizing the `datepicker` widget and extending `options`. We still have the option of providing a custom date format for each individual widget, and this route could save us a lot of potentially repetitive `dateFormat` options.

Making a full-sized calendar widget

The typical use for the `datepicker` widget is to augment a standard form input field. When the field comes into focus, it's then that we want to display the actual datepicker for the user. This makes sense if we're following the standard usage pattern for the widget—to pick dates. This is why, after all, it's called a datepicker.

But we could, however, take advantage of some flexibility afforded by the theme framework and perform a few minor tweaks to display a larger calendar. Not necessarily for the purpose of picking a date as input, but as a large window into date/time related information. The changes we need to make to the widget are merely to scale the inline display up in size.

Getting ready

The datepicker widget already knows how to display itself inline. We just need to call the datepicker constructor on a `div` element instead of an `input` element. So we'll use this basic markup:

```
<div class="calendar"></div>
```

And a plain old `datepicker()` invocation:

```
$(function() {
    $( ".calendar" ).datepicker();
});
```

The rest of the work is performed in the theme adjustments.

How to do it...

The goal of adjusting the datepicker CSS is to make it scale up in size. The idea is to make the widget look more like a calendar and less like a form input field helper. The calendar is already displayed inline, so let's just include this new CSS on the page.

```
.ui-datepicker {
    width: 500px;
}

.ui-datepicker .ui-datepicker-title {
    font-size: 1.3em;
}

.ui-datepicker table {
    font-size: 1em;
}
```

```
.ui-datepicker td {
    padding: 2px;
}

.ui-datepicker td span, .ui-datepicker td a {
    padding: 1.1em 1em;
}
```

With that, we have a scaled up calendar widget that still functions perfectly fine as a datepicker, as we haven't altered any functionality with the widget.

How it works...

The first thing we're doing with these new style declarations is increasing the width of the calendar display to `500px`. This could be any number we choose that best fits the user interface we happen to be developing. Next, we're upping the title section—the month and the year—in terms of the font size. We're also increasing the font size of all the weekdays and month numbers, as well as providing more padding between the month day slots. We have the space now, we might as well use it. Finally, the `padding` set on the `td span` and `td a` elements fixes the height of the entire calendar; otherwise, the aspect ratio would be way out of whack. This is another number that we would want to fiddle with on a per-application basis in order to get it right.

Displaying month-to-month effects

When the datepicker selector is shown, we're typically displaying one month at a time for the user. If the user needs to navigate backward through time, they do so using the previous month button. Likewise, they can move forward through time using the next month button. The datepicker widget just empties out the datepicker `div` when this happens, regenerates some HTML for the calendar and inserts that. This all happens very quickly, essentially instantaneously as far as the user is concerned.

Let's liven up this month-to-month navigation a little bit by injecting some effects into the datepicker internals.

Getting ready

We can use any datepicker widget for this experiment, but it's probably more straightforward to just use an inline datepicker display instead of using a text `input`. That way, the datepicker is there when the page loads and we don't need to open it. Inline datepickers are created using a `div` element.

```
<div class="calendar"></div>
```

How to do it...

We'll extend the datepicker widget as follows to allow for the jQuery `fadeIn()` and `fadeOut()` functions to be applied while we're adjusting the the current month.

```
(function( $, undefined ) {

$.extend( $.datepicker, {

    _updateDatepicker: function( inst ) {

        var self = this,
            _super = $.datepicker.constructor.prototype;

        inst.dpDiv.fadeOut( 500, function() {
            inst.dpDiv.fadeIn( 300 );
            _super._updateDatepicker.call( self, inst );
        });

    }

});
```

```
}) ( jQuery );

$(function() {
    $( ".calendar" ).datepicker();
});
```

Now when the user clicks on the next or previous arrow buttons at the top of the calendar, we'll see that the widget fades out and fades back in with a new calendar month layout.

How it works...

The first thing you'll notice about this code is that it doesn't extend the datepicker widget using the typical widget factory machinery. That's because the default implementation of the datepicker hasn't yet moved over to the new widget factory way of doing things. But that doesn't stop us from extending the widget to suit our needs.

> The datepicker widget is complicated—much more so than most others within the framework. There are many considerations the core jQuery UI team must entertain before such a drastic change is introduced. The plan, as of writing, is that the datepicker widget we'll be a product of the widget factory, just like every other widget in a future release.

We're using the jQuery `extend()` function on the `$.datepicker` object. This object is a singleton instance of the `Datepicker` class, which is what we're interested in for the sake of brevity. The `_updateDatepicker()` method is what we're targeting in this customization. The default datepicker implementation uses this method to update the contents of the datepicker `div`. So we want to override it. In our version of the method, we're hiding `inst.dpDiv` using `fadeOut()`. Once that completes, we call `fadeIn()`. The `_super` variable is a reference to the `Datepicker` class used to defined the widget. As `$.datepicker` is an instance, the only way to access the `Datepicker` prototype is through `$.datepicker.constructor.prototype`. The reason we need the `Datepicker` prototype is so that we can call the original `_updateDatepicker()` method once we've finished with our effects, as it performs several other tasks related to configuring the display.

Appointment reminders as tooltips

Datepicker widgets help users select the proper date for an `input` field, or serve as a basic display. In either case, wouldn't it be useful if we could provide the user with some more context? That is, if I'm using the datepicker to select the date on a form, it would be helpful to know that when I move the mouse pointer over a day in the calendar, I've got something going on that day. Maybe I should pick something else.

In this section, we'll look at extending the capabilities of the datepicker widget to allow for specifying reminders that appear as tooltips. These get passed, as an option, to the datepicker constructor and probably originated within the application somehow, perhaps from the user's profile in the database.

How to do it...

We'll use a simple inline datepicker for this example with `<div class="calendar"></div>` as the target markup.

Let's extend the datepicker's capabilities by accepting an array of reminder objects, and creating tooltips for them. A reminder object is just a plain JavaScript object with `date` and `text` fields. The date tells the datepicker where in the calendar the tooltip should be placed.

```javascript
(function( $, undefined ) {

$.extend( $.datepicker, {

    _updateDatepicker: function( inst ) {

        var settings = inst.settings,
            days = "td[data-handler='selectDay']",
            $target = inst.dpDiv,
            _super = $.datepicker.constructor.prototype;

        _super._updateDatepicker.call( this, inst )

        if ( !settings.hasOwnProperty( "reminders" ) ) {
            return;
        }

        $target.find( days ).each( function( i, v ) {

            var td = $( v ),
                currentDay = new Date(
                    td.data( "year" ),
                    td.data( "month" ),
                    td.find( "a" ).html()
                );

            $.each( settings.reminders, function( i, v ) {

                var reminderTime = v.date.getTime(),
                    reminderText = v.text,
                    currentTime = currentDay.getTime();

                if ( reminderTime == currentTime ) {
```

```
                    td.attr( "title", reminderText ).tooltip();
                }

            });

        });

    }

});

})( jQuery );

$(function() {
    $( ".calendar" ).datepicker({
        reminders: [
            {
                date: new Date(2013, 0, 1),
                text: "Happy new year!"
            },
            {
                date: new Date(2013, 0, 14),
                text: "Call in sick, case of the Mondays"
            },
            {
                date: new Date(2013, 1, 14),
                text: "Happy Valentine's Day!"
            }
        ]
    });
});
```

Now, when you move the mouse pointer over the provided reminder dates in the datepicker widget, you should see the provided text as a tooltip:

How it works...

Let's take a step back and think about the data passed to the reminders parameter, and what we've done with it. The value passed is an array of objects, each with `date` and `text` attributes. The text is what we want to display in the tooltip, and the date tells the datepicker where to place the tooltip. So we take this value and compare it against the dates rendered in the datepicker calendar.

All the customized work is done in our own implementation of the `_updateDatepicker()` method. This method is called every time the calendar is rendered. This includes switching from month to month. We use our reference to the original datepicker implementation in `_super` to call the `_updateDatepicker()` method. Once that has completed, we can perform our customizations. We first check if the reminders parameter has been supplied, otherwise, our work is done.

Next, we find and iterate over each `td` element that represents a day in the currently-displayed month. For each day, we construct a JavaScript `Date` object representative of the table cell—we'll need this to compare against each reminder entry. Finally, we iterate over each reminder object in the `reminders` parameter. If we're on the date that this reminder should be displayed, we construct the tooltip widget after setting the `title` attribute of the `td` element.

Restricting the date range

Your application may need to restrict allowable date selections for limiting the date range. Perhaps this is predicated on some other condition being true or event being triggered. Thankfully, we have enough flexibility to handle the most common selection-restricted configurations of the widget.

Getting ready...

We'll use the basic input element markup for our datepicker widget:

```
<div>
    <label for="start">Start:</label>
    <input id="start" type="text" size="30"/>
</div>
```

How to do it...

We'll create our datepicker widget as follows, using the `minDate` and `maxDate` options.

```
$(function() {

    $( "input" ).datepicker({
        minDate: new Date(),
        maxDate: 14
    });

});
```

When we activate the datepicker widget by clicking on the `input` field, you'll notice that only a specific range of days are selectable.

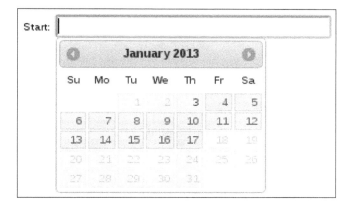

How it works...

Both the `minDate` and `maxDate` options accept a variety of formats. In our example here, we gave the `minDate` option a `Date` object, representing today. This means that the user cannot select any dates prior to today. Further, we don't want to allow the user to select any dates past two weeks into the future. This is easy to specify by giving the `maxDate` option a delta of `14` days.

There's more...

The restricted date range of a given datepicker instance doesn't have to be statically defined. The actual range might depend on something dynamic within the UI such as another datepicker selection.

Let's take a look at how we might go about restricting the date range depending on the selection of another date. We'll create two datepicker widgets. When the user selects a date in the first widget, the second widget is enabled with an updated range restriction. The user cannot select a date before the first datepicker.

Here is the markup we'll use for the two datepickers:

```
<div>
    <label for="start">Start:</label>
    <input id="start" type="text" size="30"/>
</div>

<div>
    <label for="start">Stop:</label>
    <input id="stop" type="text" size="30"/>
</div>
```

And here is the code to create our two datepicker widgets:

```
$(function() {

    function change ( e ) {

        var minDate = $( this ).datepicker( "getDate" );

        $( "#stop" ).datepicker( "enable" );
        $( "#stop" ).datepicker( "option", "minDate", minDate );

    }

    $( "#start" ).datepicker()
                    .change( change );

    $( "#stop" ).datepicker( { disabled: true } );

});
```

By default, the #stop datepicker is disabled because we need to know what the minDate value should be.

Start:	
Stop:	

But once the user makes a selection in the #start datepicker, we can make a selection in the #stop datepicker—we just can't select anything prior to the selection we made in the #start datepicker.

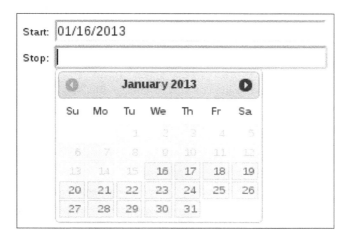

The `#start` datepicker enables and updates the `#stop` datepicker when a selection is made. It enables the widget and passes the value of `getDate` as the `minDate` option. This forces the user in one direction based on a prior selection.

Hiding the input field

The goal of the datepicker widget is to populate a text `input` element once the user makes a selection. So the widget has two uses for the `input` element. First, it listens for `focus` events on the `input` element. This is how it knows when to display the calendar selector. Second, once the selection is made, the `input` element value is updated to reflect the date in the chosen format.

Presenting the user with an `input` element would work fine in the majority of cases. But perhaps for some reason, an input doesn't suit your UI well. Maybe we need a different approach to displaying the calendar and storing/displaying the selection.

In this section, we'll look at an alternative approach to just using the datepicker `input` element. We'll use a **button** widget to trigger the calendar display, and we'll disguise the `input` element as being something else.

Getting ready

Let's use the following HTML for this example. We'll lay out four date sections where the user needs to press a button in order to interact with the datepicker widget.

```
<div>

    <div class="date-section">
        <label>Day 1:</label>
```

```
        <button>Day 1 date</button>
        <input type="text" readonly />
    </div>

    <div class="date-section">
        <label>Day 2:</label>
        <button>Day 2 date</button>
        <input type="text" readonly />
    </div>

    <div class="date-section">
        <label>Day 3:</label>
        <button>Day 3 date</button>
        <input type="text" readonly />
    </div>

    <div class="date-section">
        <label>Day 4:</label>
        <button>Day 4 date</button>
        <input type="text" readonly />
    </div>

</div>
```

How to do it...

The first thing we'll need to make our date sections work as expected is some CSS. This is important not only for laying out the UI we're building, but also for disguising the input element, so that the user doesn't know it's there.

```css
div.date-section {
    padding: 5px;
    border-bottom: 1px solid;
    width: 20%;
}

div.date-section:last-child {
    border-bottom: none;
}

div.date-section label {
    font-size: 1.2em;
    font-weight: bold;
    margin-right: 2px;
}
```

```
div.date-section input {
    border: none;
}
```

Now we'll write the JavaScript code necessary to instantiate the datepicker and button widgets.

```
$(function() {

    var input = $( "div.date-section input" ),
        button = $( "div.date-section button" );

    input.datepicker({
        dateFormat: "DD, MM d, yy"
    });

    button.button({
        icons: { primary: "ui-icon-calendar" },
        text: false
    });

    button.click( function( e ) {
        $( this ).next().datepicker( "show" )
    });

});
```

With that, we now have four date sections where the user can click on the date button to the right of the label and get the calendar displayed. They pick a date, and the calendar is hidden. You'll notice that our CSS styles have hidden the `input` element.

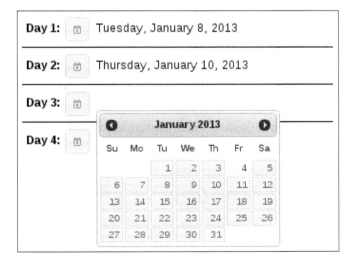

How it works...

Most of the CSS style rules in this example are required for laying out the UI components, `label`, `buttons`, and `input`. You'll notice that until a date is selected, the input isn't visible. This is because it has no text value yet, and because we've removed `border` in our `div`. `date-section` input CSS selector.

The first thing our JavaScript code does on page load is create datepicker widgets for each input element. We pass a custom string along to the `dateFormat` option too. For each date section, we have a button. We use the button widget here to create a calendar icon button that when clicked, displays the calendar. We do this by calling `datepicker( "show" )`.

Additional calendar data and controls

The datepicker widget has a variety of additional data and control options that may be exposed by the developer using the widget. These are simple Boolean configuration options that turn on the data or the control.

Getting started

Let's prepare two `div` elements with which we can create two inline datepicker instances.

```
<div>
    <strong>Regular:</strong>
    <div id="regular"></div>
</div>

<div>
    <strong>Expanded:</strong>
    <div id="expanded"></div>
</div>
```

How to do it...

Let's create the two datepicker widgets. We're creating two widgets so that we can contrast the differences between a regular datepicker and one with expanded data and controls.

```
$(function() {

    $( "#regular" ).datepicker();

    $( "#expanded" ).datepicker({
        changeYear: true,
        changeMonth: true,
```

```
            showButtonPanel: true,
            showOtherMonths: true,
            selectOtherMonths: true,
            showWeek: true
        });

    });
```

Now you can see the differences between the two rendered datepickers. The latter has been expanded with additional controls and data.

How it works...

All we've done with the expanded `datepicker` instance is turn on some features that are turned off by default. These are as follows:

- `changeYear`: This enables the year drop-down menu.
- `changeMonth`: This enables the month drop-down menu.
- `showButtonPanel`: This enables the **Today** and **Done** buttons at the bottom of the calendar.
- `showOtherMonths`: This enables days being displayed from adjacent months.
- `showWeek`: This enables the week-of-the-year column in the calendar.

5
Adding Dialogs

In this chapter, we will cover the following recipes:

- ▸ Applying effects to dialog components
- ▸ Waiting for API data to load
- ▸ Using icons in the dialog title
- ▸ Adding actions to the dialog title
- ▸ Applying effects to dialog resize interactions
- ▸ Using modal dialogs for messages

Introduction

The dialog widget gives UI developers a tool with which they can present the user with forms or other pieces of information without disrupting what is currently on the page; dialogs create a new context. Out-of-the-box, developers can do a lot with dialog options, and many of these capabilities are turned on by default. This includes the ability to resize the dialog, and move it around on the page.

In this chapter, we'll address some common pitfalls of dialog usage typical in any web application. There is often a need to adjust the controls of the dialog and its overall appearance; we'll touch on a few of those. We'll also look at how interacting with API data complicates dialog usage and the ways to deal with that. Finally, we can add some polish to dialog widgets by looking at the various ways in which we can apply effects to them.

Applying effects to dialog components

Out-of-the-box, the dialog widget allows developers to show animations when the dialog is opened, as well as hide animations, when closed. This animation is applied to the dialog as a whole. So, for example, if we were to specify that the show option is a fade animation, the entire dialog will fade into view for the user. Likewise, if the hide option was fade, the dialog would fade out of view instead of instantaneously disappearing. To liven up this show and hide behavior, we could operate on individual dialog components. That is, instead of applying show and hide effects to the dialog as a whole, we could apply them to the individual parts inside the widget, like the title bar and the button pane.

How to do it...

The dialog we're going to create here is just about as simple as they come in terms of content. That is, we're going to only specify some basic title and content strings for the dialog in the HTML.

```html
<div title="Dialog Title">
    <p>Basic dialog content</p>
</div>
```

In order to turn this idea of animating individual dialog components into reality, we'll have to extend the dialog widget in a few places. In particular, we're going to animate the title bar, at the top of the widget, as well as the button pane near the bottom. Here is what the JavaScript code looks like:

```javascript
(function( $, undefined ) {

$.widget( "ab.dialog", $.ui.dialog, {

    _create: function() {

        this._super();

        var dialog = this.uiDialog;

        dialog.find( ".ui-dialog-titlebar" ).hide();
        dialog.find( ".ui-dialog-buttonpane" ).hide();

    },

    open: function() {

        this._super();
```

```
        var dialog = this.uiDialog;

        dialog.find( ".ui-dialog-titlebar" ).toggle( "fold", 500 );
        dialog.find( ".ui-dialog-buttonpane" ).toggle( "fold", 500 );

    },

    close: function( event, isCallback ) {

        var self = this,
            dialog = this.uiDialog;

        if ( isCallback ) {
            this._super( event );
            return;
        }

        dialog.find( ".ui-dialog-titlebar" ).toggle( "fold", 500 );
        dialog.find( ".ui-dialog-buttonpane" ).toggle( "fold", 500,
function(){
            self.element.dialog( "close", event, true );
        });

    }

});

})( jQuery );

$(function() {

    $( "div" ).dialog({
        show: "fade",
        hide: "scale",
        buttons: {
            Cancel: function() {
                $( this ).dialog( "close" );
            }
        }
    });

});
```

When you open the page, you'll see the individual dialog components fade into view, independent of the `fade` animation we've specified for the dialog as a whole. Once visible, the dialog should look something like this:

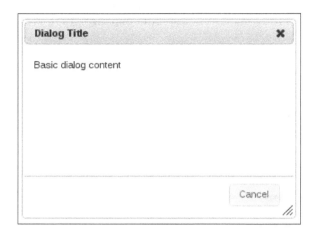

You'll also notice that the `scale` effect isn't applied until the `fade` effect is applied to the title bar and button panes.

How it works...

This code is one of those exceptions to the rule where we're not providing a mechanism with which to turn off our new extended functionality. That is, we have hard-coded changes in our custom implementation of some dialog methods that cannot be turned off by supplying an option value. However, the exception is made in an effort to trade-off complexity for desired functionality. Chances are that this type of custom animation work would happen as part of a specific project requirement, and not as a generalized extension of the dialog widget capabilities.

The first thing we change about the default dialog implementation is in the `_create()` method, where we hide the `.ui-dialog-titlebar` and `.ui-dialog-buttonpane` components. This is done after calling the `_super()` method, which is responsible for creating the basic dialog components. Even if the dialog is set to open automatically with the `autoOpen` option, the `_create()` method doesn't actually display it. So, we can hide the title bar and button pane without the user noticing it.

The reason we've hidden the two components is because we would like to apply a display effect once the dialog opens. The next method, `open()`, that we're overriding does exactly that. It first calls the `_super()` method, which initiates the effect for displaying the dialog (in our case, we've told it to fade on display). We then use the `fold` effect on the title bar and on the button pane.

You'll notice that we don't wait for any animations to complete before starting the next. The dialog display animation is started, followed by the title bar and the button pane. All three could be executing at the same time, potentially. The reason we've done it this way is to retain the correct layout of the dialog. The last method to override is the `close()` method. This introduces an interesting work-around we must use in order to get `_super()` to work in a callback. Even with the `self` variable in the enclosing scope, we have problems calling the `_super()` method inside the callback. So, we use the widget element and pretend like we're calling `.dialog( "close" )` from outside of the widget. The `isCallback` argument tells the `close()` method to call `_super()`, and return. The reason we need a callback to begin with is that we don't actually want to execute the dialog hide animation until we've finished animating the button pane.

Waiting for API data to load

More often than not, the dialog widget needs to load data from an API. That is, not all dialogs are composed of static HTML. They need data from the API to construct some of the elements using API data, such as `select` element options.

Loading data from the API and building the resultant elements isn't the issue; we do this all the time. The challenge comes when we try to perform these activities within the dialog context. We don't necessarily want to display the dialog until the data has been loaded from the API, and the UI components used to display them inside the dialog components have been built. Ideally, we would block the dialog from displaying until the components displayed by the dialog are ready.

This is especially tricky with remote API functionally, where it is impossible to predict latency issues. Furthermore, the dialog may depend on more than one API call, each populating its own UI component in the dialog.

Getting ready...

To implement a solution for the API data problem, we'll need some basic HTML and CSS to define the dialog and its content. We'll have two empty `select` elements in the dialog. This is what the HTML looks like:

```
<div id="dialog" title="Genres and Titles">
    <div class="dialog-field">
        <label for="genres">Genres:</label>
        <select id="genres"></select>
        <div class="ui-helper-clearfix"></div>
    </div>

    <div class="dialog-field">
        <label for="titles">Titles:</label>
```

```
            <select id="titles"></select>
            <div class="ui-helper-clearfix"></div>
        </div>
    </div>
```

And, this is the supporting CSS for the previous code:

```
.dialog-field {
    margin: 5px;
}

.dialog-field label {
    font-weight: bold;
    font-size: 1.1em;
    float: left;
}

.dialog-field select {
    float: right;
}
```

How to do it...

We'll give the dialog widget the ability to block while waiting on API requests by extending the widget with a new option. This option will allow us to pass in an array of deferred promises. A promise is an object used to track the state of an individual Ajax call. With a collection of promises, we're able to implement complex blocking behavior using simple code like this:

```
(function( $, undefined ) {

$.widget( "ab.dialog", $.ui.dialog, {

    options: {
        promises: []
    },

    open: function( isPromise ) {

        var $element = this.element,
            promises = this.options.promises;

        if ( promises.length > 0 && !isPromise ) {

            $.when.apply( $, promises ).then( function() {
```

```
                    $element.dialog( "open", true );
                });


            }
            else {

                this._super();

            }

        },

    });

    })( jQuery );

    $(function() {

        var repos = $.ajax({
            url: "https://api.github.com/repositories",
            dataType: "jsonp",
            success: function( resp ) {
                $.each( resp.data, function( i, v ) {
                    $( "<option/>" ).html( v.name )
                                    .appendTo( "#repos" );
                });
            },
        });

        var users = $.ajax({
            url: "https://api.github.com/users",
            dataType: "jsonp",
            success: function( resp ) {
                $.each( resp.data, function( i, v ) {
                    $( "<option/>" ).html( v.login )
                                    .appendTo( "#users" );
                });
            }
        });

        $( "#dialog" ).dialog({
            width: 400,
            promises: [
                repos.promise(),
```

```
                          users.promise()
                  ]
          });

      });
```

Once the API data is returned, for both the calls, the dialog is displayed and should look something like this:

How it works...

Let's start by looking at the document ready handler where we're actually instantiating the dialog widget. The first two variables defined here, `repos` and `users`, are `$.Deferred` objects. These represent two API calls we're making to the GitHub API. The objective of these calls is to populate the `#repos` and the `#users` `select` elements, respectively. These `select` elements make up part of our `#dialog` content. The `success` option specified in each Ajax call is a callback that performs the work of creating the `option` elements, and placing them in the `select` element.

Without customizing the dialog widget, these two API calls would work just fine. The dialog would open, and eventually, the options would appear in the `select` elements (after the dialog has already opened). You'll notice, however, that we're passing an array of `deferred.promise()` objects to the dialog. This is a new capability we've given to the dialog widget. A deferred object, simply put, allows developers to postpone the consequences of some action that might take a while to complete, such as an Ajax call. A promise is something we get from a deferred object that lets us compose some criteria that says when a complex sequence, such as making multiple Ajax calls, is complete.

The custom `promises` option we've added to the dialog widget is used in our implementation of the `open()` method. It is here that we can make use of these promises. Essentially, we're making a transaction out of one or more promise objects passed to the dialog—once they've all completed or resolved to use the jQuery terminology, we can open the dialog. We do so by passing the array of promise objects to the `$.when()` function, which calls the `open()` method on the dialog. However, a complication arises here that we must deal with. We can't call `_super()` from within a callback function because the core widget machinery doesn't understand how to find the parent widget class.

So, we have to pretend as though we're calling `open()` from outside of the widget. We do this by using `self.element`, and the additional `isPromise` parameter, instructing our custom `open()` implementation on how to behave.

Using icons in the dialog title

With some dialogs, depending on the nature of the application and the content of the dialog itself, it may be beneficial to place an icon beside the dialog title. This could be beneficial in the sense that it provides additional context to the user. For example, an edit dialog might have a pencil icon, whereas a user profile dialog might contain a person icon.

Getting ready...

To illustrate adding an icon to the title bar of the dialog widget, we'll use the following as our basic HTML:

```html
<div id="dialog" title="Edit">
    <div>
        <label>Field 1:</label>
        <input type="text"/>
    </div>
    <div>
        <label>Field 2:</label>
        <input type="text"/>
    </div>
</div>
```

How to do it...

The first thing we'll need to define is a custom CSS class used to properly align the icon once we place it in the title bar of the dialog. The CSS looks like this:

```css
.ui-dialog-icon {
    float: left;
    margin-right: 5px;
}
```

Next, we have our JavaScript code to customize the dialog widget by adding a new `icon` option as well as creating an instance of the widget using our HTML as the source:

```javascript
(function( $, undefined ) {

$.widget( "ab.dialog", $.ui.dialog, {

    options: {
```

```
            icon: false
        },

    _create: function() {

        this._super();

        if ( this.options.icon ) {

            var iconClass = "ui-dialog-icon ui-icon " +
                            this.options.icon;

            this.uiDialog.find( ".ui-dialog-titlebar" )
                        .prepend( $( "<span/>" ).addClass( iconClass
));

        }

    },

});

})( jQuery );

$(function() {

    $( "#dialog" ).dialog({
        icon: "ui-icon-pencil",
        buttons: {
            Save: function() { $( this ).dialog( "close" ) }
        }
    });

});
```

The resulting dialog, when opened, should look something like the following:

How it works...

For this particular dialog instance, we would like to display the pencil icon. Our `icon` option we've added to the dialog widget allows the developer to specify an icon class from the theme framework. In this case, it's `ui-icon-pencil`. The new `icon` option has a default value of `false`.

We're overriding the default dialog implementation of the `_create()` method so that we can inject a new `span` element into the dialog title bar if the `icon` option was provided. This new `span` element gets the icon class passed as the new option value, in addition to the `ui-dialog-icon` class, which is used to position the icon we defined earlier.

Adding actions to the dialog title

By default, the dialog widget provides the user with one action that doesn't require developer intervention—the close button in the title bar. This is a universal action that applies to almost any dialog, as users would expect to be able to close them. Additionally, it isn't by accident that the close dialog action button is an icon positioned in the top-right corner of the dialog. This is a standard location and action in graphical windowing environments as well, in addition to other actions. Let's take a look at how we might go about extending the actions placed in the title bar of the dialog widget.

How to do it...

For this demonstration, we only need the following basic dialog HTML:

```
<div id="dialog" title="Dialog Title">
    <p>Basic dialog content</p>
</div>
```

Next, we'll implement our dialog specialization that adds a new option and some code that creates a new dialog instance using that option:

```
(function( $, undefined ) {

$.widget( "ab.dialog", $.ui.dialog, {

    options: {
        iconButtons: false
    },

    _create: function() {

        this._super();
```

```
                    var $titlebar = this.uiDialog.find( ".ui-dialog-titlebar" );

                    $.each( this.options.iconButtons, function( i, v ) {

                        var button = $( "<button/>" ).text( v.text ),
                            right = $titlebar.find( "[role='button']:last" )
                                            .css( "right" );

                        button.button( { icons: { primary: v.icon }, text: false }
    )
                                .addClass( "ui-dialog-titlebar-close" )
                                .css( "right", (parseInt(right) + 22) + "px" )
                                .click( v.click )
                                .appendTo( $titlebar );

                    });

                }

            });

        })( jQuery );

        $(function() {

            $( "#dialog" ).dialog({
                iconButtons: [
                    {
                        text: "Search",
                        icon: "ui-icon-search",
                        click: function( e ) {
                            $( "#dialog" ).html( "<p>Searching...</p>" );
                        }
                    },
                    {
                        text: "Add",
                        icon: "ui-icon-plusthick",
                        click: function( e ) {
                            $( "#dialog" ).html( "<p>Adding...</p>" );
                        }
                    }
                ]
            });

        });
```

When this dialog is opened, we'll see the new action buttons we passed to the dialog in the top-right corner, as shown in the following screenshot:

How it works...

We've created a new option for the dialog called `iconButtons`. This new option expects an array of objects, where each object has attributes related to an action button. Things like the text, the icon class, and the click event have to be executed when the user opens the dialog, and clicks on the button.

The bulk of the work in this customization takes place in our version of the `_create()` method. Here, we iterate over each button supplied in the `iconButtons` option. The first thing we do when inserting a new button into the title bar is create the `button` element. We also get the width of the last action button added using the `.ui-dialog-titlebar [role='button']:last` selector (this is needed to compute the horizontal placement of the action button).

Next, we bind the `click` event as specified in the button configuration. For each button in the array that we're adding, we want it placed to the left of the previous button. So when we first start iterating over the `iconButtons` array, the default close action is the last button in the title bar. Since the CSS structure requires a fixed right value, we have to compute it. And to do that, we need the value of the last button in the list.

Applying effects to dialog resize interactions

By default, the dialog widget allows users to resize by dragging the resize handle. The actual resize capability is provided by the `resizable()` interaction widget setup internally by the dialog when the `resizable` option is `true`. Let's take a look at how to gain access to the internal resizable component, so that we can use the `animate` feature. This option, when set on a resizable component, delays the redrawing of the resized component until the user has stopped dragging the resize handle.

Getting ready...

We only need simple dialog HTML for this demonstration, like this:

```
<div id="dialog" title="Dialog Title">
    <p>Basic dialog content</p>
</div>
```

How to do it...

Let's add a new option to the dialog widget called `animateResize`. When this option is `true`, we'll turn on the `animate` option of the internal resizable interaction widget.

```
(function( $, undefined ) {

$.widget( "ab.dialog", $.ui.dialog, {

    options: {
        animateResize: false
    },

    _makeResizable: function( handles ) {
        handles = (handles === undefined ? this.options.resizable :
handles);
        var that = this,
            options = this.options,
            position = this.uiDialog.css( "position" ),
            resizeHandles = typeof handles === 'string' ?
                handles :
                "n,e,s,w,se,sw,ne,nw";

        function filteredUi( ui ) {
            return {
                originalPosition: ui.originalPosition,
                originalSize: ui.originalSize,
                position: ui.position,
                size: ui.size
            };
        }

        this.uiDialog.resizable({
            animate: this.options.animateResize,
            cancel: ".ui-dialog-content",
            containment: "document",
            alsoResize: this.element,
```

```
                    maxWidth: options.maxWidth,
                    maxHeight: options.maxHeight,
                    minWidth: options.minWidth,
                    minHeight: this._minHeight(),
                    handles: resizeHandles,
                    start: function( event, ui ) {
                        $( this ).addClass( "ui-dialog-resizing" );
                        that._trigger( "resizeStart", event, filteredUi( ui )
);
                    },
                    resize: function( event, ui ) {
                        that._trigger( "resize", event, filteredUi( ui ) );
                    },
                    stop: function( event, ui ) {
                        $( this ).removeClass( "ui-dialog-resizing" );
                        options.height = $( this ).height();
                        options.width = $( this ).width();
                        that._trigger( "resizeStop", event, filteredUi( ui )
);

                        if ( that.options.modal ) {
                            that.overlay.resize();
                        }
                    }
                })
                .css( "position", position )
                .find( ".ui-resizable-se" )
                .addClass( "ui-icon ui-icon-grip-diagonal-se" );
        }

    });

})( jQuery );

$(function() {

    $( "#dialog" ).dialog({
        animateResize: true
    });

});
```

When this dialog is created and displayed, you'll be able to resize the dialog, observing that the actual resize is now animated.

How it works...

We've added the `animateResize` option to the dialog and provided it with a default value of `false`. To actually perform this capability, we've completely overwritten the `_makeResizable()` method, which the dialog widget uses internally when the dialog is created. In fact, we've taken the internal code for `_makeResizable()` and changed only one thing about it—`animate: this.options.animateResize`.

This is slightly redundant, copying all this code for turning on a simple feature like animating the dialog resize interaction. Indeed, it isn't the ideal solution. A better approach would be to call the `_super()` version of `_makeResizable()`, then just turn on animate by calling `this.uiDialog.resizable( "option", "animate", true )`. But at the time of this writing, this doesn't behave as expected. Our alternative route, even though it involves redundant code, just goes to show the flexibility of the widget factory. If this animation quality were a real requirement of a user interface, we quickly found a work-around with a negligible trade-off.

Using modal dialogs for messages

The dialog widget has a `modal` option reserved for when we need to focus the user's attention on just one thing. This option displays the dialog while preventing the user from interacting with the rest of the user interface. They have no choice but to take notice. This goes without saying, the modal dialog should be used sparingly, especially if you want to use it to broadcast messages to the user.

Let's look at how we can strip down the dialog in order to construct a generic notification tool in our application. It is a modal dialog in essence that is used for those cases where we cannot let the user continue what they're doing without ensuring they've seen our message.

Getting ready...

Here is what the HTML we'll need for this example looks like. Notice that the #notify div, which will become a dialog widget, has no content as our new notify widget will supply some.

```
<div id="notify"></div>

<button id="show-info">Show Info</button>
<button id="show-error">Show Error</button>
```

How to do it...

Let's go ahead and define a new notify widget, capable of displaying both error and information messages to the user like this:

```
(function( $, undefined ) {

$.widget( "ab.notify", $.ui.dialog, {

    options: {
        modal: true,
        resizable: false,
        draggable: false,
        minHeight: 100,
        autoOpen: false,
        error: false
    },

    open: function() {

        var error = this.options.error,
            newClass = error ? "ui-state-error" :
                               "ui-state-highlight",
            oldClass = error ? "ui-state-highlight" :
                               "ui-state-error";

        this.element.html( this.options.text );

        this.uiDialog.addClass( newClass )
                .removeClass( oldClass )
                .find( ".ui-dialog-titlebar" )
                .removeClass( "ui-widget-header ui-corner-all" );

        this._super();
```

```
        },

    });

    })( jQuery );

    $(function() {

        $( "#notify" ).notify();

        $( "#show-info, #show-error" ).button();

        $( "#show-info" ).click( function( e ) {

            $( "#notify" ).notify( "option", {
                error: false,
                text: "Successfully completed task"
            });

            $( "#notify" ).notify( "open" );

        });

        $( "#show-error" ).click(function( e ) {

            $( "#notify" ).notify( "option", {
                error: true,
                text: "Failed to complete task"
            });

            $( "#notify" ).notify( "open" );

    })
```

The two buttons we've created here are used for demonstrating the notify widget's capabilities. If you click the #show-info button, you'll see the following informational message:

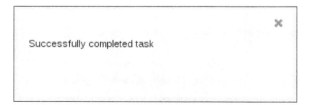

If you click the `#show-error` button, you'll see this error message:

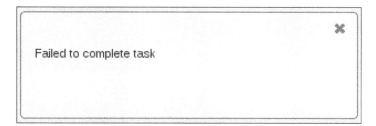

How it works...

The `notify` widget we've just created inherits all of the dialog widget's capabilities. The first thing we define in our widget is the available options. In this case, we're extending the `options` object of the dialog widget, and adding some new options. You'll notice, too, that we're providing some updated default values for the dialog options such as turning `modal` on and turning `draggable` off. Every notify instance will share these defaults, so it doesn't make much sense to have to define them each and every time.

The `open()` method belongs to the dialog widget, and we're overriding it here to implement custom functionality that inserts the text of the notification message into the dialog content. We also set the state of the dialog based on the `error` option. If this is an error message, we apply the `ui-state-error` class to the entire dialog. If the `error` option is `false`, we apply the `ui-state-highlight` class. Finally, the dialog title bar component is stripped down by removing some classes, since we're not using it in the message display.

In the application code, the first thing we're creating is an instance of the notify widget. We then create the demo buttons and bind the `click` event to the functionality that will display an error message or an informational one, depending on which button is clicked.

6
Making Menus

In this chapter, we will cover:

- ▶ Creating sortable menu items
- ▶ Highlighting the active menu item
- ▶ Using effects with menu navigation
- ▶ Building menus dynamically
- ▶ Controlling the position of submenus
- ▶ Applying themes to submenus

Introduction

The jQuery UI **menu** widget takes a list of links and presents them as a cohesive menu to the user by handling navigation in submenus, as well as applying classes from the theme framework. We can customize the menu to a certain degree, using just the default options available. In other cases, such as when we would like the menu items sortable, we can easily extend the widget.

Creating sortable menu items

The menu widget, by default, preserves the order of the listed elements used to create the menu items. It means that if the creator of the HTML used in the menu widget were to change the ordering, this would be reflected in the rendered menu. This is good for the developers because it gives us control over how we would like the items to be presented to the user. But, perhaps the user has a better idea on how the menu items should be ordered.

By combining the menu widget with the **sortable interaction** widget, we can provide the user with that flexibility. However, with this new capability, we will have to address another question; preserving the order chosen by the user. It is great if they can arrange the menu items how they see fit, but it is not so great if they have to repeat the same process every time the page loads. So we'll look, as well, at preserving the sorted menu order in a cookie.

Getting ready

Let's use the following HTML code for our menu widget. This will create a menu with four items, all at the same level:

```
<ul id="menu">
    <li id="first"><a href="#">First Item</a></li>
    <li id="second"><a href="#">Second Item</a></li>
    <li id="third"><a href="#">Third Item</a></li>
    <li id="fourth"><a href="#">Fourth Item</a></li>
</ul>
```

How to do it...

Let's now look at the JavaScript used to extend the menu widget in order to provide the sortable behavior..

```
(function( $, undefined ) {

$.widget( "ab.menu", $.ui.menu, {

    options: {
        sortable: false
    },

    _create: function() {

        this._super();

        if ( !this.options.sortable ) {
            return;
        }

        var $element = this.element,
            storedOrder = $.cookie( $element.attr( "id" ) ),
            $items = $element.find( ".ui-menu-item" );
        if ( storedOrder ) {
```

```
        storedOrder = storedOrder.split( "," );

        $items = $items.sort( function( a, b ) {

            var a_id = $( a ).attr( "id" ),
                b_id = $( b ).attr( "id" ),
                a_index = storedOrder.indexOf( a_id ),
                b_index = storedOrder.indexOf( b_id );

            return a_index > b_index;

        });

        $items.appendTo( $element );

    }

    $element.sortable({

        update: function( e, ui ) {

            var id = $( this ).attr( "id" ),
                sortedOrder = $( this ).sortable( "toArray" )
                                        .toString();

            $.cookie( id, sortedOrder );

        }

    });

    },

});

})( jQuery );

$(function() {
    $( "#menu" ).menu( { sortable: true } );
});
```

If you look at this menu in the browser, you'll notice that you can drag the menu items into any order you like. Additionally, if you were to refresh the page, you'll see that the ordering has been preserved.

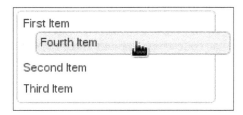

How it works...

The menu instance we're creating in this example is given a `sortable` option value of `true`. This is a new option we've added to the menu widget. The bulk of our extension work is performed in our own rendition of the `_create()` method. The first thing we do here is call the original implementation of the method since we want the menu to be created as usual; we do it by using the `_super()` method. From here on out, we're maintaining the sort order of the menu items.

If the `sortable` option doesn't evaluate to `true`, we exit, not having anything to do. In the event that this option is `true`, and we need to sort our menu items, we attempt to load a cookie, using the ID of this menu. The value of this cookie is stored in a variable called the `storedOrder`, because that's exactly what it represents; the stored order as dictated by the user. If the user has sorted the menu, we store the order of the menu items in the cookie. For example, the cookie value might look like `second, fourth, first, third`. These are the IDs of the menu items. When we split the comma-separated list, we have an array of menu items, in the correct order.

Finally, we have to apply the sortable interaction widget to the menu. We pass the sortable configuration a function that is used when the sort order is updated. It is here that we use the `toArray()` method of the sortable widget to serialize the sort order of the menu items and it is here that we update the cookie value, using the menu ID.

There are two things to note about the use of cookies in this example. First, we're using the cookie jQuery plugin. This plugin is small and in widespread use around the internet. However, it is worth mentioning that the plugin does not ship with jQuery or jQuery UI and your project will have to manage this dependency.

The second thing to note is with regards to the localhost domain. The cookie storage functionality will not work locally in all browsers. In other words, it works fine if viewed from a web server. If you really need to test this code in the Google Chrome browser, you can get around it as I did using Python. In an operating system console, run the following code:

```
python -m SimpleHTTPServer
```

Highlighting the active menu item

With menu widgets, depending on how the items are configured, the only way to tell if an item is active is when the page URL changes as a result of an item being clicked on. The menu items don't give any obvious indication that anything has actually happened. For example, the item in a menu, once clicked, could change the visual state. This is especially helpful if the developer is using the menu widget as a navigational tool in the user interface. Let's look at how we can extend the capabilities of the menu widget in order to provide this functionality using parts from the theme framework.

Getting ready

We'll use the following HTML code for our menu example here. Notice that this particular menu has a nested submenu:

```
<ul id="menu">
    <li><a href="#first">First Item</a></li>
    <li><a href="#second">Second Item</a></li>
    <li><a href="#third">Third Item</a></li>
    <li>
      <a href="#forth">Fourth Item</a>
      <ul>
        <li><a href="#fifth">Fifth</a></li>
        <li><a href="#sixth">Sixth</a></li>
      </ul>
    </li>
</ul>
```

How to do it...

In order to highlight the active menu item, we're going to need to extend the theme framework with a few additional rules.

```
.ui-menu .ui-menu-item {
    margin: 1px 0;
    border: 1px solid transparent;
}

.ui-menu .ui-menu-item a.ui-state-highlight {
    font-weight: normal;
    margin: -px;
}
```

Next, we'll extend the menu widget itself with a new `highlight` option and the necessary functionality.

```javascript
(function( $, undefined ) {

$.widget( "ab.menu", $.ui.menu, {

    options: {
      highlight: false
    },

    _create: function() {

      this._super();

        if ( !this.options.highlight ) {
          return;
        }

        this._on({
          "click .ui-menu-item:has(a)": "_click"
        });

    },

    _click: function( e ) {

      this.element.find( ".ui-menu-item a" )
        .removeClass( "ui-state-highlight" );

        $( e.target ).closest( ".ui-menu-item a" )
          .addClass( "ui-state-highlight ui-corner-all" );

    }

});

})( jQuery );

$(function() {
    $( "#menu" ).menu( { highlight: true });
});
```

If you were to look at this menu, you'd notice that once you select a menu item it would remain in the highlighted state.

How it works...

The CSS rules we've defined here are necessary for the `ui-state-highlight` class to function properly when applied to a menu item. First, with the `.ui-menu .ui-menu-item` selector, we're setting the `margin` to something that will appropriately align the menu item once the `ui-state-highlight` class is applied. We're also giving each menu item an invisible `border` so that the mouse enter and mouse leave events don't nudge the menu items out of place. The next selector, `.ui-menu .ui-menu-item a.ui-state-highlight`, applies to our menu items once we've applied the `ui-state-highlight` class to them. The rules also control positioning, and prevent the menu from becoming misaligned.

Moving over to the JavaScript code, you can see that we've provided the menu widget with a new `highlight` option. In our custom implementation of the `_create()` method, we call the original implementation of the same method before proceeding to add our event handlers. The `_on()` method, defined by the base jQuery UI widget, is used here to bind our event handler to the `click .ui-menu-item:has(a)` event; the same event used internally in the menu widget. Inside this handler, we remove the `ui-state-highlight` class from any menu items it might already be applied to. Finally, we add the `ui-state-highlight` class to the menu item just clicked on, along with the `ui-corner-all` class, which gives the element rounded corners as defined by the theme properties.

Using effects with menu navigation

There are several approaches we could take when it comes to applying effects to the menu widget. Where could we apply effects in the menu widget? The user hovers their mouse pointer over the menu items, which results in a state change. The user expands a submenu. These two actions are the main interactions we could improve visually with some animation. Let's look at how we can address these effects using as little JavaScript as possible in favor of using CSS transitions. Transitions are an emerging CSS standard in so far, that not all browsers support them using standard syntax yet. In the spirit of progressive enhancement, however, applying CSS in this way means that the basic menu functionality will work just fine even in browsers that don't support it. And we can side-step having to write an overwhelming amount of JavaScript to animate the menu navigation.

Getting ready

For this example, we can use any standard menu HTML code. Ideally, it should have a submenu so we can observe the transitions applied to their expansion.

How to do it...

First, let's define the CSS required for the transitions we want to be applied to the menu items and submenus as they change state.

```
.ui-menu-animated > li > ul {
    left: 0;
    transition: left 0.7s ease-out;
    -moz-transition: left .7s ease-out;
    -webkit-transition: left 0.7s ease-out;
    -o-transition: left 0.7s east-out;
}

.ui-menu-animated .ui-menu-item a {
    border-color: transparent;
    transition: font-weight 0.3s,
      color 0.3s,
      background 0.3s,
      border-color 0.5s;
    -moz-transition: font-weight 0.3s,
        color 0.3s,
        background 0.3s,
        border-color 0.5s;
    -webkit-transition: font-weight 0.3s,
        color 0.3s,
        background 0.3s,
        border-color 0.5s;
    -o-transition: font-weight 0.3s,
        color 0.3s,
        background 0.3s,
        border-olor 0.5s;
}
```

Next, we'll introduce some modifications to the menu widget itself, necessary to control the animation capabilities of any given menu instance.

```
(function( $, undefined ) {

$.widget( "ab.menu", $.ui.menu, {
```

```
    options: {
        animate: false
    },

    _create: function() {

        this._super();

        if ( !this.options.animate ) {
            return;
        }

        this.element.find( ".ui-menu" )
                    .addBack()
                    .addClass( "ui-menu-animated" );

    },

  _close: function( startMenu ) {

        this._super( startMenu );

        if ( !this.options.animate ) {
            return;
        }

        if ( !startMenu ) {
            startMenu = this.active ? this.active.parent() : this.
element;
        }

        startMenu.find( ".ui-menu" ).css( "left", "" );

        }


});

})( jQuery );

$(function() {
    $( "#menu" ).menu( { animate: true } );
});
```

Now, if you were to look at this menu in your browser and start interacting with it, you would notice the smooth transitions in applying the hover state. You'd also notice that the transition applied to the submenus appears to slide them to the right when expanded.

How it works...

First, let's consider the CSS rules that define the transitions we're seeing applied to the `menu` widget. The `.ui-menu-animated > li > ul` selector applies transitions to submenus. The first property declared, `left: 0`, is merely an initializer that allows a certain browser to work better with transitions. The next four lines define the transition itself of the left property. The menu widget, when expanding submenus, uses the position utility widget, which sets the left CSS property on the submenu. The transition we've defined here will apply changes to the left property over a `span` of `0.7` seconds, and will ease out of the transition.

The reason we have multiple transition definitions is that some browsers support their own vendor-prefixed version of the rule. So we start with the generic version, followed by the browser-specific versions. This is a common practice, and when the browser-specific rules become superfluous, we can remove them.

Following it comes the `.ui-menu-animated .ui-menu-item a` selector, which applies to each menu item. You can see that the transition here involves several properties. Each property in this transition is part of the `ui-state-hover` that we would like to be animated. The duration of the `border-color` transition is slightly longer as a result of our tweaks.

Now let's look at the JavaScript that puts this CSS to use. We've extended the menu widget by adding a new `animate` option, which will apply the above defined transitions to the widget. In our version of the `_create()` method, we call the original implementation of `_create()` then apply the `ui-menu-animated` class to the main `ul` element, and any submenus.

The extension of the `_close()` method is necessary for one reason only. This is called when a submenu is closed. However, when a submenu is first displayed, the `left` CSS property is computed by the `position` utility. The next time it is displayed, it doesn't have to compute the `left` property. This is a problem, for obvious reasons, if we're trying to animate a change in the `left` property value. So all we do to fix this is set the `left` property back to a value of `0` when the menu is closed.

Building menus dynamically

Often, the menus change during interaction with a user. In other words, we may need to extend the structure of the menu after the menu has been instantiated. Alternatively, we might not have all the necessary information available to us when building the HTML that ultimately becomes the menu widget; the menu data may only be available in **JavaScript Object Notation (JSON)** format, for instance. Let's look at how we can go about building menus dynamically.

Getting ready

We will start with the following basic menu HTML structure. Our JavaScript code will extend this.

```
<ul id="menu">
    <li><a href="#">First Item</a></li>
    <li><a href="#">Second Item</a></li>
    <li><a href="#">Third Item</a></li>
</ul>
```

How to do it...

Let's create the menu widget, and then we'll extend the structure of the menu DOM.

```
$(function() {

    var $menu = $( "#menu" ).menu(),
        $submenu = $( "<li><ul></ul></li>" ).appendTo( $menu );

    $submenu.prepend( $( "<a/>" ).attr( "href", "#" )
                                    .text( "Fourth Item" ) );

    $submenu.find( "ul" ).append(
$( "<li><a href='#'>Fifth Item</a>" ) )
                                        .append( $( "<li><a
href='#'>Sixth Item</a>" ) );

    $menu.menu( "refresh" );

});
```

Instead of just the three initial items we started off with, when you view this menu, you are now presented with the three new items we have just added.

How it works...

If we don't keep adding the new menu items in our JavaScript code, we would only see the original three items. However, we are using the core jQuery DOM manipulation tools to construct and insert a submenu. Afterward, we have to call the `refresh()` menu method, which adds the appropriate CSS classes and event handlers to the new menu items. If, for example, we moved the DOM insertion code to before the `menu` widget is instantiated, we would have no reason to call `refresh()` since the menu constructor invokes it directly.

There's more...

The above approach of inserting new items in a menu does have its drawbacks. The obvious one being that the DOM insertion code that actually constructs the new menu items and submenu isn't maintainable. Our example has hard-coded the structure, which most applications never do. Instead, we typically have at least one data source, from an API perhaps. It would be nice, if instead of hard-coding the structure, we could pass the menu widget a data source, with a standard format. The menu widget would then take care of the low-level details that we've implemented above.

Let's try and modify the code so that we shift more responsibility to the menu widget itself. We'll aim for the exact same outcome as the code above, but we'll do so by extending the menu widget, and passing in a data object that represents the menu structure. We'll use the exact same HTML structure. Here is the new JavaScript code:

```
(function( $, undefined ) {

$.widget( "ab.menu", $.ui.menu, {

    options: {
        data: false
    },

    _create: function() {

        this._super();

        if ( !this.options.data ) {
            return;
        }

        var self = this;

        $.each( this.options.data, function( i, v ) {
            self._insertItem( v, self.element );
```

```
        });

        this.refresh();

    },

    _insertItem: function( item, parent ) {

        var $li = $( "<li/>" ).appendTo( parent );

        $( "<a/>" ).attr( "id", item.id )
                   .attr( "href", item.href )
                   .text( item.text )
                   .appendTo( $li );

        if ( item.data ) {

            var $ul = $( "<ul/>" ).appendTo( $li ),
                self = this;

            $.each( item.data, function( i, v ) {
                self._insertItem( v, $ul );
            });

        }

    }

});

})( jQuery );

$(function() {

    $( "#menu" ).menu({
        data: [
            {
                id: "fourth",
                href: "#",
                text: "Fourth Item"
            },
            {
                id: "fifth",
                href: "#",
```

```
                        text: "Fifth Item",
                        data: [
                            {
                                id: "sixth",
                                href: "#",
                                text: "Sixth Item"
                            },
                            {
                                id: "seventh",
                                href: "#",
                                text: "Seventh Item"
                            }
                        ]
                    }
                ]
            });

    });
```

If you run this modified code, you'll see no change in outcome compared to the original code we've written above. This improvement is purely a re-factoring, turning unmaintainable code into something with a longer shelf life.

The new option we've introduced here, `data`, expects an array of menu items. The item is an object with the following attributes:

- ▶ `id`: It is the id for the menu item
- ▶ `href`: It is the href of the menu item link
- ▶ `text`: It is the item label
- ▶ `data`: It is a nested submenu

The last option is simply a nested array of menu items representing a submenu. Our modifications to the `_create()` method will iterate over the data option array, if provided, and call `_insertItem()` on each object. The `_insertItem()` method is something new we've introduced, and does not override any existing menu functions. Here, we're creating the necessary DOM elements for the passed in menu data. If this object has a nested data array, a submenu, then we create a `ul` element and recursively call `_inserItem()`, passing the `ul` as the parent.

The `data` we pass to the menu is significantly more readable and maintainable than the previous version. Passing API data, for instance, would take relatively little work now.

Controlling the position of submenus

The menu widget uses the position widget to control the destination of any submenus when visible. The default is to place the top left of the submenu to the right of the menu item that expands the submenu. But depending on the size of our menu, the depth of the submenus, and other constraints around size in our UI, we might want to use different defaults for the submenu positions.

Getting ready

We will use the following HTML structure for this submenu positioning demonstration:

```html
<ul id="menu">
        <li><a href="#first">First Item</a></li>
        <li><a href="#second">Second Item</a></li>
        <li><a href="#third">Third Item</a></li>
        <li>
          <a href="#forth">Fourth Item</a>
          <ul>
            <li><a href="#fifth">Fifth</a></li>
            <li>
              <a href="#sixth">Sixth</a>
              <ul>
                <li><a href="#">Seventh</a></li>
                <li><a href="#">Eighth</a></li>
                </ul>
                </li>
              </ul>
            </li>
          </ul
```

How to do it...

When we instantiate this menu, we will pass it a position option as follows:

```html
<ul id="menu">
        <li><a href="#first">First Item</a></li>
        <li><a href="#second">Second Item</a></li>
        <li><a href="#third">Third Item</a></li>
        <li>
            <a href="#forth">Fourth Item</a>
            <ul>
                <li><a href="#fifth">Fifth</a></li>
                <li>
```

```
                    <a href="#sixth">Sixth</a>
                    <ul>
                        <li><a href="#">Seventh</a></li>
                        <li><a href="#">Eighth</a></li>
                    </ul>
                </li>
            </ul>
        </li>
    </ul>
```

With all the submenus expanded our menu will look similar to that shown in the following screenshot:

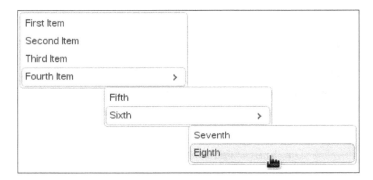

How it works...

The `position` options that we're passing to the menu widget in the preceding example are the same options we would pass directly to the position widget. The `of` option, which the position utility expects, is the active menu item or the parent of the submenu. All these options are passed to the position utility inside the `_open()` method, which is responsible for expanding submenus.

Applying themes to submenus

When the menu widget displays submenus, there is no discernible difference in appearance. That is, visually, they look just like the main menu. We wanted to present the user with a little contrast between the main menu and its children; we can do so by extending the widget to allow for custom classes to be applied to the submenus.

Getting ready

Let's use the following markup to create our menu widget with a couple submenus:

```
<ul id="menu">
        <li><a href="#">First Item</a></li>
        <li><a href="#">Second Item</a></li>
        <li><a href="#">Third Item</a></li>
        <li>
            <a href="#">Fourth Item</a>
            <ul>
                <li><a href="#">Fifth</a></li>
                <li>
                    <a href="#">Sixth</a>
                    <ul>
                        <li><a href="#">Seventh</a></li>
                        <li><a href="#">Eighth</a></li>
                    </ul>
                </li>
            </ul>
        </li>
    </ul>
```

How to do it...

We will extend the menu widget by adding a new submenuClass option and apply that class to submenus as shown in the following code:

```
(function( $, undefined ) {

$.widget( "ab.menu", $.ui.menu, {

    options: {
      submenuClass: false
    },

    refresh: function() {

      if ( this.options.submenuClass ) {

        this.element.find( this.options.menus + ":not(.ui-menu)" )
          .addClass( this.options.submenuClass );

      }

      this._super();

    }
```

```
    });

    })( jQuery );

    $(function() {
        $( "#menu" ).menu( { submenuClass: "ui-state-highlight" } );
    });
```

Here is what the submenu looks like:

How it works...

Here, we are extending the menu widget with a new `submenuClass` option. The idea being that we want to apply this class only to the submenus of the widget if supplied. We do this by overriding the `refresh()` menu method. We look for all the submenus and apply the `submenuClass` to them. You'll notice that we apply this class before calling the `_super()` method in the original implementation of this method. This is because we are searching for menus that do not have the `ui-menu` class yet. These are our submenus.

7
Progress Bars

In this chapter, we will cover the following recipes:

- ► Displaying file upload progress
- ► Animating progress changes
- ► Creating progress indicator widgets
- ► Using states to warn about thresholds
- ► Giving progressbars labels

Introduction

The **progressbar** widget is quite simple—in that it doesn't have many moving parts. In fact, it has exactly one moving part, that is, the value bar. But simplicity doesn't make the progressbar any less powerful than other widgets. We'll look at how we can leverage this simplicity throughout this chapter. The progressbar can express anything from file upload progress to server-side processes to capacity utilization.

Displaying file upload progress

It would be nice if there was a straightforward way to display the progress of a file upload using the progressbar widget. Unfortunately, we are afforded no such luxury. The uploading of a file happens between the transitions of pages. However, the necessary hacks to display the upload progress using the progressbar widgets have shrunk in size, thanks to the modern standards and browsers. Let's take a look at how we can take advantage of the `onprogress` event of the XML HTTP Request object in **Ajax** requests.

Getting ready

For this demonstration, we will create a simple form with a simple file field. Inside the form, we'll create some HTML for displaying the progressbar widget. It'll be hidden until the user initiates a file upload.

```html
<form action="http://127.0.0.1:8000/" method="POST">
    <input type="file" name="fileupload"/>
    <br/>
    <input type="submit" value="Upload"/>
    <div id="upload-container" class="ui-helper-hidden">
        <strong id="upload-value">Uploading...</strong>
        <div id="upload-progress"></div>
    </div>
</form>
```

How to do it...

The bulk of the work required to update the progressbar widget during a file upload is actually performed in the Ajax request machinery and in the `onprogress` event handler. The following code is a really good illustration of why widget designers should aim for simplicity. The resulting widget is applicable to a wide variety of contexts.

```javascript
$(function() {

    $( "#upload-progress" ).progressbar();

    $( "form" ).submit( function( e ) {

        e.preventDefault();

        $.ajax({
            url: $( this ).attr("action"),
            type: "POST",
            data: new FormData( this ),
            cache: false,
            contentType: false,
            processData: false,
            xhr: function() {

                xhr = $.ajaxSettings.xhr();

                if ( xhr.upload ) {
                    xhr.upload.onprogress = onprogress;
                }
```

```
                return xhr;

            }

        });

        return false;

    });

    var onprogress = function( e ) {

        var uploadPercent = ( e.loaded / e.total * 100 ).toFixed();

        $( "#upload-container" ).show();
        $( "#upload-value" ).text( "Uploading..." + uploadPercent +
"%" );
        $( "#upload-progress" ).progressbar( "option", "max", e.total
)
                            .progressbar( "value", e.loaded );

    };

});
```

If you run this example and actually upload a file locally at `http://127.0.0.1:8000/`, you'll want to use a large file. Smaller files will upload too fast and in too short a time. A larger file upload will enable you to see something like the following during an upload.

 Accompanying the code in this book is a minimal Python server that will serve this demo upload page and will process the file upload requests. The example can be rearranged without much effort to work with any upload server, but the Python server supplied only requires that Python be installed. Again, this isn't a requirement, but it's just a handy server if you're eager to see the client code in action.

How it works...

The goal of this example is to update the progressbar widget in real time, as the file upload progress changes. There are several plugins that will provide this capability, but if you're writing a jQuery UI application, you might as well standardize on the progressbar widget. The first thing we do, once the document is ready, is create the progressbar widget used to display the file upload progress. `#upload-container` is initially hidden using the `ui-helper-hidden` class, as we don't need to display the progress of an upload until an upload is actually taking place.

Next, we set up our event handler for the `submit` event of our upload form. This handler, before doing anything else, prevents the default form submission from taking place. We're essentially substituting our own behavior for the default form submission implemented by the browser. The reason we need to override this behavior is so that we stay on the page, and apply updates to our progressbar widget.

Next, we set up the `$.ajax()` call that actually sends our selected files to the server. We take the `url` argument from the form itself. The next several arguments are prerequisites to sending multipart form data, including selected files, as part of an Ajax request. The `xhr` option is where we supply a function that returns the `xhr` object used internally by the `$.ajax()` function. This is our opportunity to hijack the `xhr` object and attach additional behavior to it. We're mainly interested in adding new behavior to the `onprogress` event.

After we've made sure that the upload object, an instance of `XMLHttpRequestUpload`, actually exists, we can define our `onprogress` event handler function.

Firstly, we calculate the actual upload percentage, using the `loaded` and `total` properties of the event. Next, we show the progress container and update the percentage label using the value in `uploadPercent`. Finally, we make sure that the `max` option of the upload progressbar widget is set to `total`, and we set the current value of the progressbar using the `value()` method.

Animating progress changes

The progressbar widget changes its visual appearance each time the `value` or the `max` option is set. For example, the default value for `value` is `0` and the default value for `max` is `100`. So when the progressbar widget is displayed with these values, we don't actually see the graphical bar, yet that depicts the progress percentage. However, setting the `value` option will update this bar. If the bar is already visible, a change in the `value` option results in a change of the width for the progressbar. These changes, using the default progressbar implementation, simply change the widget instantaneously. Let's look at how we can modify the widget to support a smooth transition between progressbar values.

How to do it...

We'll use the following simple markup as the basis of our progressbar widget instance:

```
<div id="progress"></div>
```

And, here is the JavaScript used to customize the progressbar widget in order to support animating changes in progress:

```
(function( $, undefined ) {

$.widget( "ab.progressbar", $.ui.progressbar, {

    options: {
        animate: false
    },

    _refreshValue: function() {

        if ( !this.options.animate ) {
            return this._super();
        }

        var value = this.value(),
            percentage = this._percentage();

        if ( this.oldValue !== value ) {
            this.oldValue = value;
            this._trigger( "change" );
        }

        this.valueDiv.toggle( value > this.min )
.toggleClass( "ui-corner-right",
value === this.options.max )
                            .stop( true, true )
                            .animate( { width: percentage.toFixed( 0
) + "%" }, 200 );

            this.element.attr( "aria-valuenow", value );

    }

});

})( jQuery );
```

```
$(function() {

    $( "#progress" ).progressbar( { animate: true } );

    var timer;

    var updater = function() {
        var value = $( "#progress" ).progressbar( "value" ) + 10,
            maximum = $( "#progress" ).progressbar( "option", "max" );

        if ( value >= maximum ) {
            $( "#progress" ).progressbar( "value", maximum );
            return;
        }

        $( "#progress" ).progressbar( "value", value );
        timer = setTimeout( updater, 700 );

    };

    timer = setTimeout( updater, 700 );

});
```

This example includes an updater that will increment the progressbar value at every 0.7 seconds interval. You'll notice the smooth width transition applied as the value changes. To contrast this change with the default behavior, set the `animate` option to `false`. You'll now start to really notice the visual jumps the bar makes each time the value is updated.

How it works...

Our example code extends the progressbar widget by adding a new `animate` option. The new `animate` option defaults to `false`. The other change we're introducing to the progressbar widget is the new implementation of the `_refreshValue()` method, which is called internally by the widget any time the `value` option changes. This method is responsible for making the visual width change on the `div` element `progress`. This is representative of the progress between `value` and `max`.

Much of this code is borrowed from the original implementation of `_refreshValue()`, as we're only making minor changes. First, we check if the `animate` option we've added to the widget has a `true` value. If not, we just continue with the original implementation. Otherwise, we use the same code, but make a slight adjustment with how the width is applied. Then, we're calling `stop( true, true )` to complete the current animation and to clear the animation queue. Next, instead of using the `width()` function as does the original implementation, we're setting the width by calling `animate()`.

There's more...

As always, we're not limited to using the jQuery `animate()` function to apply effects to the visual transitions between progressbar values. Instead of the `animate()` function, we could apply CSS transitions to progressbar values. Of course, the drawback is that not all browsers support CSS transitions, and we get into vendor-specific style rules. Nonetheless, let's compare the previous approach with that of using the CSS styles to animate the progressbar.

We will use the same markup, but we'll introduce the following styles into the page:

```
.ui-progressbar-animated > .ui-progressbar-value {
    transition: width 0.7s ease-out;
    -moz-transition: width .7s ease-out;
    -webkit-transition: width 0.7s ease-out;
    -o-transition: width 0.7s east-out;
}
```

And, here are the necessary changes to the JavaScript code. It looks similar to the previous code.

```
(function( $, undefined ) {

$.widget( "ab.progressbar", $.ui.progressbar, {

    options: {
        animate: false
    },

    _create: function() {

        this._super();

        if ( !this.options.animate ) {
            return;
        }

        this.element.addClass( "ui-progressbar-animated" );

    }

});

})( jQuery );
```

```
$(function() {

    $( "#progress" ).progressbar( { animate: true } );

    var timer;

    var updater = function() {

        var value = $( "#progress" ).progressbar( "value" ) + 10,
            maximum = $( "#progress" ).progressbar( "option", "max" );

        if ( value >= maximum ) {
            $( "#progress" ).progressbar( "value", maximum );
            return;
        }

        $( "#progress" ).progressbar( "value", value );
        timer = setTimeout( updater, 700 );

    };

    timer = setTimeout( updater, 700 );

});
```

Running this example will not look all that different from the previous implementation of the `animate` option. The transition will behave much in the same way. The key difference here is that we are extending the theme framework. We have introduced a new CSS class for the progressbar widget—`ui-progressbar-animated`. The selector, `.ui-progressbar-animated > .ui-progressbar-value`, applies to the progressbar value `div`, the one that changes width. And, this is exactly what our new styles do. They transition width property value changes over a span of 0.7 seconds.

The JavaScript code is the chief benefactor of this approach simply because there is less change in the progressbar widget. For instance, we're no longer overriding the `_refreshValue()` method. Instead, we're overriding `_create()`, and adding the `ui-progressbar-animated` class to the element if the `animated` option is `true`. This is how our new styles are put into action. The rest of the JavaScript that instantiates the widget and the value updater is no different from the previous example.

Creating progressindicator widgets

The progressbar widget is intended to show the progress of some process. The end goal is the max option specified when creating the widget, which defaults to 100. If we know the size of the data we are processing ahead of time, we would use the max option to reflect this end goal. However, we are sometimes faced with the scenario where we have some processing to do on the client; or, we are waiting for some backend process to complete and send a response back to the client. For example, the user has initiated a backend task using the API, and they're now waiting for a response. The bottom line is, we want to illustrate to the user that progress is being made, and we just don't know how much progress has been made.

To display the fact that progress is being made, despite not knowing how much progress, we need an indicator widget. We can write our own widget to achieve this, extending the progressbar widget, since we can reuse many components there.

How to do it...

For our progressindicator widget, we will use the same HTML as we would for a basic progressbar widget.

```html
<div id="indicator"></div>
```

Next, we have some slight adjustments to make in the progressbar CSS styles. These apply to the value bar inside the progressbar div. We're removing the border and the margin since this looks better when sliding the value bar back and forth.

```css
.ui-progressbar > .ui-progressbar-value {
    border: none;
    margin: 0px;
}
```

Now, we come to the implementation of the progressindicator widget. This code will also create an instance of our progressindicator widget.

```js
(function( $, undefined ) {

$.widget( "ab.progressindicator", $.ui.progressbar, {

    _create: function() {

        this._super();
        this.value( 40 );
        this.element.removeClass( "ui-corner-all" );
        this.valueDiv.removeClass( "ui-corner-right ui-corner-left" );
```

```
            var self = this,
                margin = ( this.element.innerWidth() - this.valueDiv.
    width() ) + "px";

            var _right = function() {

                self.valueDiv.animate(
                    { "margin-left": margin },
                    { duration: 1000, complete: _left }
                );

            };

            var _left = function() {

                self.valueDiv.animate(
                    { "margin-left": "0px" },
                    { duration: 1000, complete: _right }
                );

            };

            _right();

        },

        _destroy: function() {

            this.valueDiv.stop( true, true );
            this._super();

        }

    });

})( jQuery );

$(function() {

    $( "#indicator" ).progressindicator();

});
```

If you look at this progressindicator widget in the browser, you will see that it animates the value bar of the progressbar widget by sliding it back and forth, indicating that something is happening.

How it works...

We have created a new progressindicator widget that inherits the progressbar widget capabilities. The goal behind the progressindicator widget is to take the progress value bar div, set a width on it, and slide it back and forth within the progressbar container div. Visually, this indicates that something is taking place behind the scene. This type of graphical depiction of an activity is universally reassuring to users, as it gives the sense that something is happening, and the application isn't broken.

The first method we're overriding in the definition of the new progressindicator widget is the _create() method of the progressbar. Here, we're calling the original constructor of the progressbar widget, since we need all the UI components in place before we start making changes. Next, we use the value() method to give the value bar div a width. We're hardcoding this value in the progressindicator() constructor simply because the developer using this widget has no need to change it; we only need to set the width of the element. To further simplify this widget, we're removing the corner classes from the elements. We could leave them, but then we would have to handle several corner cases when it comes to animating the bar, as we're after a simple widget here, one that requires no configuration on behalf of the developer using the widget.

Still inside the _create() method, we define two utility functions for executing animation. As you may have guessed, the _right() function slides the progress value bar to the right while the _left() function slides it to the left. We're calling the animate() jQuery function on the valueDiv property of this widget. The _right() function slides the value div to the right by updating the margin-left value. You'll notice that the margin variable is defined locally inside _create(). This is done by calculating how much space we have to the right of the value div, which means that we set this value as the margin-left to slide it over to the right. To slide it back to the left again, we simply set the margin-left CSS property back to 0px in the _left() function.

The animation is bootstrapped by calling _right() at the bottom of the _create() method. The progress indicator animation loop happens by passing _left() as a callback to the initial animation. Likewise, we pass _right() as the animation completion callback inside the _left() function. This process will continue until the widget is destroyed. The _destroy() method is overridden by our widget simply to make sure that all animations stop immediately. This includes any queued animations waiting to execute. We then continue destroying the widget by calling the original _destroy() implementation.

There's more...

One advantage to our progressindicator widget is that it provides a very simple API. You can create and destroy the widget as needed, without having to deal with any intermediary steps. Ideally, this widget would have a very short lifespan, perhaps as little as one second (barely enough time to see one animation cycle). Sometimes, however, things may take a little longer. If this widget were to display for an extended period of time, it could pose a problem to the application. The jQuery `animate()` function wasn't designed to run animations in an infinite loop. Nor is our widget designed to be displayed for extended periods of time. The problem is that `animate()` uses timers and can really eat away at the CPU cycles on the client. Not only could this be disruptive to our application, but for others running on the user's machine too.

Despite this being a relatively minor concern, let's look at an alternative implementation of our progressindicator widget, one that uses CSS animations. Here is how we would define our animations in the CSS:

```css
.ui-progressindicator > .ui-progressbar-value {
    border: none;
    margin: 0px;
    animation: indicator 2s ease-in-out infinite;
    -moz-animation: indicator 2s ease-in-out infinite;
    -webkit-animation: indicator 2s ease-in-out infinite;
}

@keyframes indicator {
    0%   { margin-left: 0px; }
    50%  { margin-left: 108px; }
    100% { margin-left: 0px; }
}

@-moz-keyframes indicator {
    0%   { margin-left: 0px; }
    50%  { margin-left: 108px; }
    100% { margin-left: 0px; }
}

@-webkit-keyframes indicator {
    0%   { margin-left: 0px; }
    50%  { margin-left: 108px; }
    100% { margin-left: 0px; }
}

@-o-keyframes indicator {
    0%   { margin-left: 0px; }
    50%  { margin-left: 108px; }
    100% { margin-left: 0px; }
}
```

And, here is the modified JavaScript implementation of our `progressindicator` widget that knows how to make use of the previous CSS:

```
(function( $, undefined ) {

$.widget( "ab.progressindicator", $.ui.progressbar, {

  _create: function() {

        this._super();
        this.value( 40 );
        this.element.addClass( "ui-progressindicator" )
                  .removeClass( "ui-corner-all" );
        this.valueDiv.removeClass( "ui-corner-right ui-corner-left" );

    },

    _destroy: function() {

        this.element.removeClass( "ui-progressindicator" );
        this._super();

    }

});

})( jQuery );

$(function() {

    $( "#indicator" ).progressindicator();

});
```

Now, if you view this modified version of the widget in your browser, you should see a nearly identical result when compared with the previous implementation. The key difference of course being that the animation is specified in the CSS and executed directly by the browser. The browser can handle these types of CSS animations much more efficiently than the JavaScript based counterparts. The browser only needs to read the animation specification once, and then it runs the animation internally, using native code as opposed to executing JavaScript, and directly manipulating the DOM. We could run this version all day, and the browser would happily chug along.

But this version of progressindicator isn't without its pitfalls. Firstly, let's take a closer look at the CSS. The very fact that we're relying on CSS animations to begin with isn't the best bet given the disparity in browser adoption. Here, we're getting ourselves into a browser vendor prefix mess with our style. Support, in general, isn't too bad though, as IE is the only browser that doesn't support CSS animations; but the definition of the animations are straightforward. In the `.ui-progressindicator > .ui-progressbar-value` selector, we are specifying that the indicator animation will run for 2 seconds and will repeat infinitely. The `@keyframes` indicator animation specifies how the `margin-left` property itself changes.

In JavaScript, you will notice that the code itself is much simpler. This is because it now has much less responsibility. Mainly, it needs to add the `ui-progressindicator` class to the widget's DOM element on creation, and remove the class on destruction. You will also notice that there is no longer a margin calculation taking place in the JavaScript code that implements the widget. We have instead moved these numbers to the CSS that defines the widget animation as hard-coded values. Again, this is simply a trade-off that the widget designer must consider. We are exchanging higher maintenance costs in the CSS for more efficient animations, and questionable browser support for our widget for simpler JavaScript.

Using states to warn about thresholds

The progressbar widget isn't restricted to marking the progression toward some end point. It can also be used as a marker for utilization of some resource. For example, your application might allow the user to store 100 MB worth of image data. It might make sense to show them how much of this capacity is currently in use. The progressbar widget is an ideal solution for graphically depicting resource utilization scenarios such as these. Taking things a step further, we might also want to warn the user about utilization thresholds. That is, at a certain percentage, the resource is getting near capacity, but the user still has time to do something about it.

Getting ready

For this demonstration, we will create two simple `div` elements for the two progressbar widgets we want to display:

```
<span>CPU:</span>
<div id="cpu-utilization"></div>
<span>Memory:</span>
<div id="memory-utilization"></div>
```

How to do it...

Here is the JavaScript code that extends the progressbar widget, providing a new option for specifying threshold values:

```
(function( $, undefined ) {

$.widget( "ab.progressbar", $.ui.progressbar, {

    options: {
        threshold: 0
    },

  _percentage: function() {

        var percentage = this._super(),
            threshold = this.options.threshold;

        if ( threshold <= 0 ) {
            return percentage;
        }

        if ( percentage > threshold ) {
            this.valueDiv.addClass( "ui-state-error" );
        }
        else {
            this.valueDiv.removeClass( "ui-state-error" );
        }

        return percentage;

    },

});

})( jQuery );

$(function() {

    $( "#cpu-utilization" ).progressbar( { threshold: 80 } );
    $( "#memory-utilization" ).progressbar( { threshold: 85 } );

    setInterval(function() {
        var cpu = Math.floor( ( Math.random() * 100 ) + 1 ),
            memory = Math.floor( ( Math.random() * 100 ) +1 );

        $( "#cpu-utilization" ).progressbar( "value", cpu );
        $( "#memory-utilization" ).progressbar( "value", memory );

    }, 1300);

});
```

We instantiate two progressbar widgets here and launch a basic timer interval that changes the value of both the progressbar widgets after every 1.30 seconds. If you look at this example in your browser, you will notice that one or both progressbar widgets will enter the error state because the value has surpassed the supplied threshold value.

How it works...

The new `threshold` option we've added to the progressbar widget is a number expressed as a percentage. This is the threshold of the progressbar at which the state changes in order to give the user a visual warning. This is achieved by overriding the `_percentage()` method. Here, we get the actual percentage value by calling the original implementation of `_percentage()` and storing it in `percentage`. We then make sure that the `threshold` value is nonzero and that the calculated percentage is greater than the `threshold` value. The `_percentage()` method is called internally by the progressbar widget each time the value is updated, and the visual display changes. So in our implementation of `_percentage()`, if we're over the threshold, we add the `ui-state-error` class to the `valueDiv` element, the graphical bar inside the progress bar that moves from left to right. Otherwise, we're below the threshold, and must be sure to remove the `ui-state-error` class.

Once we've created the two widgets, we're using `setInterval()` to continuously assign a random value to both the progressbars. You can sit back and watch how the progressbar widgets change state depending on whether the data fed into them crosses over the thresholds that we've specified. In this case, the `#cpu-utilization` progressbar has a threshold of `80` percent, while the `#memory-utilization` progressbar has a threshold of `85%`.

Giving progressbars labels

The graphical bar that changes width to reflect the progress percentage does a fine job. The power of the progressbar widget is in the ability to see, at a glance, how much progress has been made, or how much of a resource is being utilized. But there are times when we could use some accuracy with regard to the percentage, that is, a label showing the underlying percentage.

The progressbar widget has the ability to display the label inside the progressbar container, which is more intuitive than displaying the percentage label outside of the widget. Let's look at how we can extend the theme CSS, supply additional markup to the widget, and extend the progressbar to take advantage of these new additional features in order to display the label.

How to do it...

We'll create the HTML for our two progressbar widgets first.

```
<span>Network:</span>
<div id="network-utilization">
    <div class="ui-progressbar-label"></div>
</div>
<span>Storage:</span>
<div id="storage-utilization">
    <div class="ui-progressbar-label"></div>
</div>
```

Next, we'll add the CSS class required by the progressbar label.

```
.ui-progressbar-label {
    float: left;
    width: 100%;
    text-align: center;
    margin-top: 5px;
    font-weight: bold;
}
```

Finally, we'll extend the progressbar widget itself, tying together this new HTML and the new CSS.

```
(function( $, undefined ) {

$.widget( "ab.progressbar", $.ui.progressbar, {

    _create: function() {
        this.$label = this.element.find( ".ui-progressbar-label" );
        this._super();

    },

    _destroy: function() {

        this.$label.remove();

        this._super();

    },

    _refreshValue: function() {
```

```
                    this.$label.text( this._percentage().toFixed( 0 ) + "%" );
                    this._super();

        },

    });

})( jQuery );

$(function() {

    $( "#network-utilization" ).progressbar({
        value: 746586112,
        max: 1073741824
    });

    $( "#storage-utilization" ).progressbar({
        value: 24696061952,
        max: 107374182400
    });

});
```

You can now view these two progressbars in the browser, and you'll notice that the two labels, showing the percentage value, are positioned in the center of the widget.

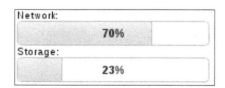

How it works...

By default, the progressbar widget does not support labels, and so we have to place the label `div` inside the progressbar `div`. We also give this new label `div` the `ui-progressbar-label` class, which is consistent with the jQuery UI theme naming convention. This class actually serves two purposes: inside the widget customizations that we have introduced, we use this class to search for the label `div` and to apply label styles.

The CSS rules specified in `ui-progressbar-label` help to position the label text in the middle of the progressbar element. We give the label `div` a width of `100%` and align the text horizontally using the `text-align` property. Finally, we make the `font-weight` of the label `bold` in order to stand out; otherwise, it is difficult to see it against the background of the progressbar.

The customized JavaScript implementation of the progressbar widget that we've introduced here overrides the `_create()` method. We create a new instance variable called `labelDiv`, which stores a reference to our new element. We then call the original `_create()` implementation and the constructor carries on as normal, creating the value `div` beside our new label element. We're also overriding the `_refreshValue()` method in order to update the content of the `labelDiv`. The `_refreshValue()` method gets invoked internally by the widget any time the value changes and the progressbar widget needs to update the value display. We're extending this behavior by updating the `labelDiv` value using the `_percentage()` number, before resuming with the original implementation of `_refreshValue()`.

There's more...

One potential issue we may encounter with this approach to implementing progressbar labels is the fact that we have to change the HTML structure. This violates the DRY principle, because every label `div` we are adding, for each progressbar widget we create, is exactly the same. Further, we may want to apply labels to progressbar widgets that already exist in an application. Altering the HTML in an already functional widget is not the best approach. Let's think about how we can improve the previous code.

The CSS we have created that positions and styles the label element is fine. It follows the correct naming conventions and it applies to all progressbar widget instances. What we want to change is the necessary markup used to instantiate a progressbar widget with a label displayed. The question is how. Ideally, through an option that lets the developer toggle the label on and off. The widget itself would then be responsible for inserting the label `div` where necessary since it is the same for all instances of the widget, which in turn means minimal JavaScript code.

Let's take a look at the simplified markup, following the same previous example:

```
<span>Network:</span>
<div id="network-utilization"></div>
<span>Storage:</span>
<div id="storage-utilization"></div>
```

We are now back to the original markup that the progressbar widget expects before we introduced our modifications. Now let's update the widget code to make use of this markup by adding a new option.

```
(function( $, undefined ) {

$.widget( "ab.progressbar", $.ui.progressbar, {

    options: {
        label: false
```

```
        },

    _create: function() {

        if ( !this.options.label ) {
            return this._super();
        }

        this.$label = $( "<div/>" ).addClass( "ui-progressbar-label" )
                            .appendTo( this.element );

        this._super();

    },

    _destroy: function() {

        if ( !this.options.label ) {
            return this._super();
        }

        this.$label.remove();

        this._super();

    },

    _refreshValue: function() {

        if ( !this.options.label ) {
            return this._super();
        }

        this.$label.text( this._percentage().toFixed( 0 ) + "%" );

        this._super();

    },

});

})( jQuery );

$(function() {
```

```
$( "#network-utilization" ).progressbar({
    value: 746586112,
    max: 1073741824,
    label: true
});

$( "#storage-utilization" ).progressbar({
    value: 24696061952,
    max: 107374182400
});

});
```

Here, we're extending the progressbar widget with the new `label` option, which defaults to `false`. The idea is that when this value is `true`, we insert the label `div` into the progressbar container. Our modifications to the `_create()` and `_refreshValue()` methods are largely the same as the previous code, except now we're checking if the `label` option is turned on before executing our custom behavior. As you can see, we're supplying this new label option to the #network-utilization div, but not the #storage-utilization div.

8
Using Sliders

In this chapter, we will cover:

- ▸ Controlling the size of the slider handle
- ▸ Removing the handle focus outline
- ▸ Using master sliders and child sliders
- ▸ Marking step increments
- ▸ Getting range values
- ▸ Changing the slider orientation

Introduction

The **slider** widget is almost like a progress bar that the user can manipulate. The slider gives the user a handle that can be dragged along a plane in order to produce the desired value. This is especially useful in working with form values. The slider widget, by default, has useful options such as the ability to change orientation and letting the user select a value range. In this chapter, we'll look at some of the various ways we can tweak the slider widget by adding new options, or by attaching even handler functions. We'll also look at some visual tweaks, and how slider instances can communicate with one another.

Controlling the size of the slider handle

The **slider handle** used to control the position of the slider, dragged by the mouse, is a square shape. That is, the width is the same as the height, and we may want a different shape for the slider handle. In the case of a **horizontal slider**, the default orientation, let's look at how we can override widget CSS styles to alter the shape of the slider handle in order to meet the needs of our application.

Getting ready...

The HTML we'll create is for two slider widgets. We'll also give them a label and wrap them each with container div elements to control the layout.

```html
<div class="slider-container">
    <span>Treble:</span>
    <div id="treble"></div>
</div>
<div class="slider-container">
    <span>Bass:</span>
    <div id="bass"></div>
</div>
```

How to do it...

Here is the CSS used to customize the slider handle. This overrides values defined in the widget CSS, and so should be included in the page after the jQuery UI stylesheet:

```css
.ui-slider-horizontal .ui-slider-handle {
    width: 0.8em;
    height: 1.6em;
    top: -0.48em;
}
```

And here is the JavaScript code used to create two instances of the slider widget:

```javascript
$(function() {

    $( "#treble" ).slider();
    $( "#bass" ).slider();

});
```

As a reference, here is what the two slider widgets look like before applying our custom CSS:

And here are the same two slider widgets with our custom CSS applied:

How it works...

As you can see, the handle is taller, extending farther beyond the boundary of the slider borders. This gives the user a larger surface area to click and drag the slider handle around. The exact size changes we've introduced are arbitrary, and can be tweaked on a per-application basis.

The `.ui-slider-horizontal` `.ui-slider-handle` selector overrides three properties defined in the widget CSS. The width is changed to `0.8em`, which makes it slightly thinner. The `height` property's value is changed to `1.6em`, which makes it taller. When we make the handle taller using the `height` property, we push it downward so that it no longer aligns with the slider. To compensate for the change in height, we pull it back up by decreasing the `top` value to `-0.48em`.

Removing the handle focus outline

Most browsers display a dotted or solid **outline** around an element when they receive the focus. This isn't part of the user interface style, but rather a built-in accessibility feature of the browser. This forced visual display around elements, such as the slider handle, isn't always desirable. Let's look at how we can go about removing this default browser behavior from the slider handle.

How to do it...

We can use any basic `div` element to base our sample slider widget on. So let's jump right to our custom slider widget CSS.

```css
.ui-slider-handle-no-outline {
    outline: 0;
}
```

And, now we have our customized implementation of the slider widget and an instance of our customized slider.

```javascript
(function( $, undefined ) {

$.widget( "ab.slider", $.ui.slider, {

    options: {
        handleOutline: true
    },

    _create: function() {

        this._super();

        if ( this.options.handleOutline ) {
            return;
        }

        this.handles.addClass( "ui-slider-handle-no-outline" );

    }

});

})( jQuery );

$(function() {

    $( "#slider" ).slider({
        handleOutline: false,
    });

});
```

Before we applied our changes to the slider widget, the handle had an outline that looked something like this after being dragged:

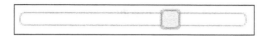

After our changes have been applied to the slider widget, our slider instance looks like this after the handle is dragged:

How it works...

We've added a new option to the slider widget called `handleOutline`. We've set this option to `true` by default because it's always a good idea to support native browser behavior out of the box. This option, when set to `false`, turns off this native border outline functionality. It does so by adding `the ui-slider-handle-no-outline` class to each handle element in the slider. There can be many handles in one slider, for example, a range slider. So in the `_create()` method, we check if the `handleOutline` option is `true`, and if so, we use the `handles` jQuery object stored as a property of this widget to apply the new class we've created.

The class itself is simple in that it only changes one property. In fact, we could have simply added the `outline` property with a value of `0` to the `ui-slider-handle` class instead of creating a new one. However, our chosen approach allows us to keep the native widget styles intact, which allows the outline browser functionality to toggle on or off for each instance of our widget. You'll also notice that the handle, even without the native browser outline, doesn't lose any accessibility because the jQuery UI state classes take care of this for us.

Using master sliders and child sliders

It is possible that your application will use some quantity that can be further decomposed into smaller values. Additionally, the user may need to control these smaller values and not just the aggregate. If we decide to use the slider widget for this purpose, we can think of the child sliders observing the changing value of the master slider. Let's take a look at how we might go about implementing such a group of sliders. We'll design an interface that allows us to allocate how much of the CPU this application is allowed to use. This is the **master slider**. We'll assume a quad-core architecture, and so we'll have four subsequent sliders that depend on, and observe, the main CPU slider.

How to do it...

Here is the HTML used to define the layout of our five sliders. Each slider has its own `div` container, mainly used to define widths and margins. Inside the `div` container, we have a label of each CPU, their current MHz allotment, and the maximum. This is where each slider widget is placed too.

```
<div class="slider-container">
    <h2 class="slider-header">CPU Allocation:</h2>
    <h2 class="slider-value ui-state-highlight"></h2>
    <div class="ui-helper-clearfix"></div>
    <div id="master"></div>
</div>

<div class="slider-container">
    <h3 class="slider-header">CPU 1:</h3>
    <h3 class="slider-value ui-state-highlight"></h3>
    <div class="ui-helper-clearfix"></div>
    <div id="cpu1"></div>
</div>

<div class="slider-container">
    <h3 class="slider-header">CPU 2:</h3>
    <h3 class="slider-value ui-state-highlight"></h3>
    <div class="ui-helper-clearfix"></div>
    <div id="cpu2"></div>
</div>

<div class="slider-container">
    <h3 class="slider-header">CPU 3:</h3>
    <h3 class="slider-value ui-state-highlight"></h3>
    <div class="ui-helper-clearfix"></div>
    <div id="cpu3"></div>
</div>

<div class="slider-container">
    <h3 class="slider-header">CPU 4:</h3>
    <h3 class="slider-value ui-state-highlight"></h3>
    <div class="ui-helper-clearfix"></div>
    <div id="cpu4"></div>
</div>
```

Next, we have some CSS styles to help align and position these components.

```css
.slider-container {
    width: 200px;
    margin: 5px;
}

.slider-header {
    float: left;
}

.slider-value {
    float: right;
}
```

Finally, we have our JavaScript code that extends the slider widget to provide developers using it with two new options, `parent` and `percentage`. When the document loads, we instantiate our CPU slider widgets and establish the appropriate relations between them using our new slider capabilities.

```javascript
(function( $, undefined ) {

$.widget( "ui.slider", $.ui.slider, {

    options: {
        parent: null,
        percentage: null
    },

    _create: function() {

        this._super();

        var parent = this.options.parent,
            percentage = this.options.percentage,
            $parent;

        if ( !( parent && percentage ) ) {
            return;
        }

        $parent = $( parent );

        this._reset( $parent.slider( "value" ) );
```

```
            this._on( $parent , {
                slidechange: function( e, ui ) {
                    this._reset( ui.value );
                }
            });

        },

        _reset: function( parentValue ) {

            var percentage = ( 0.01 * this.options.percentage ),
                newMax = percentage * parentValue,
                oldMax = this.option( "max" ),
                value = this.option( "value" );

            value = ( value / oldMax ) * newMax;

            this.option( "max", newMax );
            this.option( "value", value );

        }

    });

})( jQuery );

$(function() {

    function updateLabel( e, ui ) {

        var maxValue = $( this ).slider( "option", "max" )
                            .toFixed( 0 ),
            value = $( this ).slider( "value" )
                            .toFixed( 0 ) + " MHz" +
                                        " / " +
                                    maxValue +
                                    "MHz";

        $( this ).siblings( ".slider-value" ).text( value );

    }

    $( "#master" ).slider({
        range: "min",
```

```
            value: 379,
            min: 1,
            max: 2400,
            create: updateLabel,
            change: updateLabel
        });

        $( "#cpu1" ).slider({
            parent: "#master",
            percentage: 25,
            range: "min",
            min: 0,
            create: updateLabel,
            change: updateLabel
        });

        $( "#cpu2" ).slider({
            parent: "#master",
            percentage: 35,
            range: "min",
            min: 0,
            create: updateLabel,
            change: updateLabel
        });

        $( "#cpu3" ).slider({
            parent: "#master",
            percentage: 15,
            range: "min",
            min: 0,
            create: updateLabel,
            change: updateLabel
        });

        $( "#cpu4" ).slider({
            parent: "#master",
            percentage: 25,
            range: "min",
            min: 0,
            create: updateLabel,
            change: updateLabel
        });

    });
```

Take a look at the resulting slider widgets in the browser and adjust some of the child CPU values. You'll notice that the label updates have changed and that each CPU has its own CPU allotment.

CPU Allocation:	379 MHz / 2400MHz
CPU 1:	32 MHz / 95MHz
CPU 2:	39 MHz / 133MHz
CPU 3:	42 MHz / 57MHz
CPU 4:	39 MHz / 95MHz

Now, leaving the CPU values as they are, try adjusting the master CPU allocation slider. You'll notice that the current and maximum values for each child CPU slider change, but the ratio is preserved. This means that if we've set up CPU 1 to use 10 percent of the overall CPU allocation, it will continue to use 10 percent even if the overall allocation increases or decreases.

CPU Allocation:	1205 MHz / 2400MHz
CPU 1:	102 MHz / 301MHz
CPU 2:	124 MHz / 422MHz
CPU 3:	134 MHz / 181MHz
CPU 4:	124 MHz / 301MHz

How it works...

In each container `div` element we've created for CPU sliders, we have a header, `slider-value`, used to display both the current value of the slider in addition to the maximum value. This is an important addition we need to consider in most cases while using the slider widget. The widget is great for allowing the user to change values, but they need specific feedback that shows the result of their actions. In this example, changing the master slider updates five labels, further highlighting the need to label specific slider values outside the widget where the user can see them.

We've added two new options to the slider widget, `parent` and `percentage`. The two options are related to each other and basically translate to "the maximum value of this slider is this percentage of this parent slider value". In the `_create()` method, we're checking if both these options have an actual value before continuing, as they default to `null`. If not, we've already called the original slider constructor using the `_super()` method, and so it's safe for us to simply return.

If, on the other hand, we've been given a parent slider widget and a percentage, we call the `_reset()` method, passing it the current value of our parent slider. This will potentially update both the maximum and the current value of this widget. Once that is done, we set up our observer that watches the parent slider for changes. This is done using the `_on()` method, where we pass `parent` as the element we're listening for events on and the configuration object. This object has a `slidechange` event, which is the event we're interested in, and the callback function. Inside the callback function, we're simply calling our `_reset()` method using the updated value from the parent. It is worth noting that we must use `_on()` to register our event handler. If the child slider is destroyed, the event handler is removed from the parent.

The `_reset()` method takes a value from the parent slider and resets both the `value` and `max` options of this child slider. We're using this method both when the child is first created and when the parent value changes. The goal is to preserve the current value/max ratio. This is where the `percent` option comes into play. Since this is passed to the widget as an integer, we must multiply it by `0.01`. This is how we calculate that new maximum for this child. Once we have the new maximum value, we can scale the current value either up or down.

Finally, in the document-ready event handler where we instantiate each of the five slider widgets, we've defined a generic callback function used to update the label in each CPU `div`. This gets passed to the create and change options of each slider widget. We're also using values for our newly-defined options here. Each child slider has a unique `percentage` value of the overall CPU allocation, and each child is using #master as its `parent`.

Marking step increments

The slider widget can be passed a step value, which determines the increments by which the user can slide the handle. If unspecified, the `step` option is `1`, and the handle slides smoothly back and forth. On the other hand, if the `step` value were more pronounced, let's say `10`, we would notice the handle snapping into position as we move it. Let's take a look at how we might extend the slider widget to give the user a better feel for where these increments lie. We'll mark the increments visually using ticks.

How to do it...

We'll jump right into the custom CSS used for this widget enhancement. The underlying `div` element used for the slider element can be as simple as `<div></div>`.

```css
.ui-slider-tick {
    position: absolute;
    width: 2px;
    height: 15px;
    z-index: -1;
}
```

And here is our JavaScript code that extends the slider and creates an instance of the widget using the new `ticks` option:

```javascript
(function( $, undefined ) {

$.widget( "ab.slider", $.ui.slider, {

    options: {
        ticks: false
    },

    _create: function() {

        this._super();

        if ( !this.options.ticks || this.options.step < 5 ) {
            return;
        }

        var maxValue = this.options.max,
            cnt = this.options.min + this.options.step,
            background = this.element.css( "border-color" ),
            left;
```

```
        while ( cnt < maxValue ) {

            left = ( cnt / maxValue * 100 ).toFixed( 2 ) + "%";

            $( "<div/>" ).addClass( "ui-slider-tick" )
                         .appendTo( this.element )
                         .css( { left: left,
                                 background: background } );

            cnt += this.options.step;

        }

    }

});

})( jQuery );

$(function() {

    $( "#slider" ).slider({
        min: 0,
        max: 200,
        step: 20,
        ticks: true
    });

});
```

Looking at this slider widget, we can see that the step value we've specified, 20, is depicted using tick marks underneath the slider.

How it works...

Let's examine the additional capability we've introduced into the slider widget. We've added the `ticks` Boolean option, which is turned off by default. This option, when true, tells the widget to display the step increments using tick marks. In the `_create()` method, we're calling the original implementation of `_create()` using `_super()`, as we want the slider constructed as normal. Then, we check to see if the `ticks` option has been turned on and if the `step` value is greater than 5. If the `ticks` option has been turned on and we have a `step` value that is less than 5, they'll appear to be close to each other; so we simply don't display them.

The `cnt` counter variable controls our tick rendering loop, and is initialized to the first `step` above the `min` option. Likewise, the loop exits before the `max` option value. This is because we do not want to render tick marks at the beginning or the end of the slider, but only the mid section. The `backgroud` variable is used to extract the `border-color` CSS property from the slider widget. What we're actually doing here is transferring the theme setting to a new element we're adding to the widget. This allows the theme to be swapped, and the tick marks will change color accordingly.

Inside the `while` loop, we're creating the `div` elements that represent the tick marks. The `left` CSS property is computed to actually position the `div` so that it lines up with the slider handle as the user moves it around. The `ui-slider-tick` CSS class we're adding to the `div` element configures the common properties for each tick mark, including the `z-index`, which pushes a portion of the `div` behind the main slider bar.

Getting range values

The slider widget can be used to control a range value. So instead of moving a fixed point, that is the handle, back and forth over the slider axis, the user will move two handles back and forth. The space in between these two points represents the range value. But how do we go about computing that number? The slider widget gives us the raw data, the upper and lower bounds on the user selection. We can use these values inside our event handlers to compute the range value.

Getting ready...

We'll use just a basic slider for this demonstration, but we'll need some supporting CSS and HTML surrounding the slider so that we can display the range values as they're changed. Here is the CSS:

```css
.slider-container {
    width: 180px;
    margin: 20px;
}

.slider-container .slider-label {
    margin-bottom: 10px;
    font-size: 1.2em;
}
```

And here is the HTML:

```html
<div class="slider-container">
    <div class="slider-label">
        <span>Range Value: </span>
        <strong id="range-value"></strong>
    </div>
    <div id="slider"></div>
</div>
```

How to do it...

We'll create the `slider` instance using the following JavaScript code. Note that we're passing options specific to supporting range selections.

```javascript
$(function() {

    $( "#slider" ).slider({
        min: 0,
        max: 600,
        values: [280, 475],
        range: true,
        create: function( e, ui ) {
            var values = $( this ).data( "uiSlider" ).values();
            $( "#range-value" ).text( values[1] - values[0] );
        },
        change: function( e, ui ) {
            $( "#range-value" ).text( ui.values[1] - ui.values[0] );
        }
    });

});
```

Now when you view this slider in your browser, you'll notice that the range value is displayed as a label outside the widget. And, if you move either one of the slider handles, the label will reflect the changed range value.

Range Value: **195**

How it works...

In this example, we're creating a simple slider widget that uses a range of values instead of just a single value. We do this by passing an array of values to the widget constructor, and by passing a range value of true to the constructor as well. This is how the widget knows to use two handles instead of one, and to fill in the space between them. We're also passing the slider constructor with two event callback functions: one for the create event and the other for the change event.

The two callbacks do the same thing: they compute the range value and display it in our #range-value label. The two callbacks, however, implement the same logic in a slightly different manner. The create callback doesn't have the values array as part of the ui object, which is used to hold widget data. So, our workaround here is the use of the uiSlider data, which holds an instance of the JavaScript slider widget instance in order to access the values() method. This returns the same data that we find in the ui object passed to the change event callback.

The number we're computing here is simply the value of the first handle, minus the value of the second. For example, if we're using a slider such as this in a form, the API might not care about the two values as represented by the two slider handles, but only the range value derived by the two numbers.

Changing the slider orientation

By default, the slider widget will render horizontally. It's easy for us to change the slider orientation to a vertical layout using the `orientation` option.

How to do it...

We'll use the following HTML to define our two widgets. The first slider will be vertical while the second uses the default horizontal layout:

```
<div class="slider-container">
    <div id="vslider"></div>
</div>

<div class="slider-container">
    <div id="hslider"></div>
</div>
```

Next, we'll use the following JavaScript code to instantiate the two widgets:

```
$(function() {

    $( "#vslider" ).slider({
        orientation: "vertical",
        range: "min",
        min: 1,
        max: 200,
        value: 128
    });

    $( "#hslider" ).slider({
        range: "min",
        min: 0,
        max: 200,
        value: 128
    });

});
```

If you look at the two sliders in your browser, you can see the contrast between the vertical layout and the default horizontal layout:

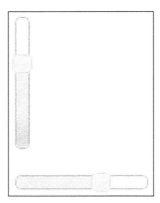

How it works...

The two slider widgets we've created here, `#vslider` and `#hslider`, are identical in terms of content. The only difference is that the `#vslider` instance is created with the `orientation` option set to `vertical`. The `#hslider` instance doesn't specify an `orientation` option and so uses the default, `horizontal`. The key difference between them is the layout as is made obvious in our example. The actual layout itself is controlled by the `ui-slider-vertical` and `ui-slider-horizontal` CSS classes, which are mutually exclusive.

Being able to control the slider orientation is valuable depending on where you want to put the widget in the context of the UI. The containing element, for example, might not have a lot of horizontal space, and so using the vertical orientation option might make good sense here. However, be careful about dynamically changing the slider orientation. The handle can sometimes break away from the slider bar. Therefore, it's best to decide on the orientation at design time.

9
Using Spinners

In this chapter, we will cover:

- ▸ Removing the input focus outline
- ▸ Formatting currencies for local cultures
- ▸ Formatting time for local cultures
- ▸ Controlling the step between values
- ▸ Specifying the spin overflow
- ▸ Simplifying the spinner buttons

Introduction

In this chapter, we'll be working with spinners. A **spinner** is nothing more than an adornment on a text `input` element. But at the same time, it's plenty more. For example, the spinner does a lot to assist with formatting numbers to local cultures as we'll see in this chapter. We'll also explore some of the options that the spinner widget ships with, and how we can expand on and improve these options. Finally, we'll take a look at some of the ways we can modify the look and feel of the spinner widget.

Removing the input focus outline

Most browsers will automatically apply an input focus outline around the `input` element when it gains the focus from the user. The element receives focus when the user either clicks the `input` element, or tabs their way there. The spinner widget is essentially an `input` element with adornments. This includes the ability to utilize the innate jQuery state classes from the CSS theme framework. While the automatic focusing behavior of the browser may work well on `input` elements by themselves, these focus rings can make the spinner look a little cluttered. Let's take a look at how we can remove the automatic focus outline, while maintaining the same level of accessibility

How to do it...

We'll create just a simple `input` element for this example. Here is what the HTML structure looks like.

```
<div class="spinner-container">
    <input id="spinner"/>
</div>
```

And, here is the custom CSS used in conjunction with our widget modifications to remove the focus outline.

```
.ui-spinner-input-no-outline {
    outline: 0;
}
```

Finally, here is our JavaScript code which alters the definition of the spinner widget, and creates an instance with no automatic outline applied by the browser.

```
(function( $, undefined ) {

$.widget( "ab.spinner", $.ui.spinner, {

    options: {
inputOutline: true
},

    _create: function() {

        this._super();

        if ( this.options.inputOutline ) {
return;
}

        this.element.addClass( "ui-spinner-input-no-outline" );
        this._focusable( this.uiSpinner );

    }
});

})( jQuery );

$(function() {

    $( "#spinner" ).spinner( { inputOutline: false } );

});
```

To give you a better idea of the change we've introduced, this is what the spinner widget we just created looked like before our modifications to the spinner definition.

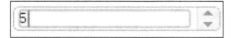

Here, you can clearly see that the `input` element has the focus, but we could do without the double border as it doesn't exactly fit nicely with our theme. Following is the modified version of the same widget in the focused state after introducing our changes.

We no longer have the focus outline, and the widget still changes its state visually when it gains focus. Except now, we're changing the appearance using state classes from the CSS theme, and not relying on the browser to do it for us.

How it works...

The CSS class that takes care of removing the outline for us, the `ui-spinner-input-no-outline` class, is easy enough to understand. We simply set the `outline` to 0 which overrides the default browser way of doing things. Our custom extension of the spinner widget knows how to make use of this class.

We've added a new `inputOutline` option to the spinner widget. This option will apply our new CSS class to the `input` element if it is set to `false`. However, `inputOutline` defaults to `true`, because we don't want to override the default browser functionality by default. Furthermore, we also don't want to necessarily override the default spinner widget functionality by default. Instead, it's safer to provider an option that when explicitly set, changes the defaults. In our implementation of the `_create()` method, we call the original implementation of the spinner constructor. Then, if the `inputOutline` option is `true`, we apply the `ui-spinner-input-no-outline` class.

Again, you may have noticed the last thing we do is apply the `_focusable()` method to the `this.uiSpinner` property. The reason being, we need to make up for the lost accessibility; the outline is no longer applied by the browser, and so we need to apply the `ui-state-focus` class when the widget gains focus. The `_focusable()` method is a simple helper defined in the base widget class, and so available to all widgets, that makes the passed elements handle the focus events. This is much simpler than dealing with the event setup and tear-down ourselves.

Formatting currencies for local cultures

It is possible to use the spinner widget in conjunction with the **Globalize** jQuery library. The Globalize library is an effort by the jQuery foundation to standardize the way jQuery projects format data for different cultures. A culture is a set of rules that formats strings, dates, and currencies according to cultural norms. For example, our application should treat German dates and currencies differently from French dates and currencies. This is how we're able to pass a `culture` value to the spinner widget. Let's look at how we can use the Globalize library with the spinner widget to format currencies to local cultures.

How to do it...

The first thing our application needs when working with several locales is to include the `globalize` libraries. Each culture is contained in its own JavaScript file.

```
<script src="globalize.js"
  type="text/javascript"></script>
<script src="globalize.culture.de-DE.js"
  type="text/javascript"></script>
<script src="globalize.culture.fr-CA.js"
  type="text/javascript"></script>
<script src="globalize.culture.ja-JP.js"
  type="text/javascript"></script>
```

Next, we'll define the HTML used to display the culture selector, made up of radio buttons, and the spinner widget, used to display currencies.

```
<div class="culture-container"></div>
<div class="spinner-container">
    <input id="spinner"/>
</div>
```

Finally, we have our JavaScript code used to populate the `culture` selector, instantiate the spinner widget, and bind the change event to the culture selector.

```
$(function() {

    var defaultCulture = Globalize.cultures.default;

    $.each( Globalize.cultures, function( i, v ) {

      if ( i === "default" ) {
        return;
      }
```

```
    var culture = $( "<div/>" ).appendTo( ".culture-container" );

    $( "<input/>" ).attr( "type", "radio" )
        .attr( "name", "cultures" )
        .attr( "id", v.name )
        .attr( "checked", defaultCulture.name === v.name )
        .appendTo( culture );

    $( "<label/>" ).attr( "for", v.name )
        .text( v.englishName )
        .appendTo( culture );

});

$( "#spinner" ).spinner({
    numberFormat: "C",
    step: 5,
    min: 0,
    max: 100,
    culture: $( "input:radio[name='cultures']:checked" )
        .attr( "id" )
});

$( "input:radio[name='cultures']" ).on
    ( "change", function( e ) {
        $( "#spinner" ).spinner( "option", "culture",
            $( this ).attr( "id" ) );
});

});
```

When you first look at this UI in your browser, you'll notice that **English** is the selected culture, and the spinner will format the currency accordingly.

But, a change in culture results in a currency format change in the spinner widget, as previously illustrated.

How it works...

The first thing we do in the JavaScript code, once the DOM is ready, is populate the `culture` selector using the `Globalize.cultures` object. The Globalize library constructs this object based on the available cultures; you'll notice a direct correlation from the available culture options and the culture scripts that we've included in the page. We store the name of the culture as the `id` attribute since this is what we pass to the spinner widget later. The `Globalize.cultures` object also has a default culture, and we use this value to determine which option is selected when the page first loads.

The spinner instance we've created uses a `numberFormat` option value of `C`. This string actually gets passed directly to the `Globalize.format()` function upon rendering of the spinner value. The next three options, `step`, `min`, and `max` are typical with any numerical spinner instances. The `culture` option, which we're setting to the selected default culture, tells the spinner widget how to format the currency. Finally, we've setup an event handling that is triggered anytime the culture selection changes. This handler will update the spinner widget to use the newly-selected culture.

Formatting time for local cultures

The spinner widget utilizes the Globalize jQuery project; an effort to standardize on data formats according to the local culture. The spinner widget utilizes this library to format its values. For example, specifying the `numberFormat` and `culture` options allow us to use the spinner widget to display currency values according to local culture. However, currency is just one value that we like to format locally; time is another. We can use the built-in Globalize capabilities only to an extent in the spinner widget for displaying time values. A little more work is required on our part to extend the widget to properly allow for time values. In fact, let's create our own time widget, based on the spinner.

How to do it...

First, let's look at the markup required for creating two time widgets in which we'll display the Toronto time and the London time. We're not showcasing the time-zone computation abilities here, simply the fact that we have two different cultures in the same UI.

```
<div class="spinner-container">
    <h3>Toronto</h3>
    <input id="time-ca" value="2:30 PM"/>
</div>

<div class="spinner-container">
    <h3>London</h3>
    <input id="time-gb" value="7:30 PM"/>
</div>
```

Next, let's have a look at the JavaScript used to define the new time widget, and create two instances of it.

```
( function( $, undefined ) {

$.widget( "ab.time", $.ui.spinner, {

    options: {
        step: 60 * 1000,
        numberFormat: "t"
    },

    _parse: function( value ) {

        var parsed = value;

        if ( typeof value === "string" && value !== "" ) {

            var format = this.options.numberFormat,
                culture = this.options.culture;

            parsed = +Globalize.parseDate( value, format );

            if ( parsed === 0 ) {
                parsed = +Globalize.parseDate( value,
                    format, culture );
            }

        }
```

```
            return parsed === "" || isNaN( parsed ) ? null :
                parsed;

        },

        _format: function( value ) {
            return this._super( new Date( value ) );
        }

    });

})( jQuery );

$(function() {

    $( "#time-ca" ).time({
        culture: "en-CA"
    });

    $( "#time-gb" ).time({
        culture: "en-GB"
    });

});
```

Looking at the two time widgets in the browser, we can see that they've been formatted to their own local culture.

How it works...

Let's first look at the two input elements used to define the time widget instances. Notice the value attribute, they both have a default time, expressed using the same format. Now, let's jump to the definition of the new time widget.

The first thing you'll notice here is that we're using the widget factory to define the time widget under the `ab` namespace. You'll also notice that we're extending the spinner widget. That's because it is essentially a spinner that we're building here, with a couple of small but important distinctions. This is actually a good example of something you'll have to consider when designing jQuery UI widget customizations that are derived from the standard set of widgets. Should you retain the original widget name, in this case spinner, or should you call it something else, in this case time? The one thing that can help you guide this decision is thinking about how this widget will be used. For example, we could have left the spinner widget intact to display these cultured time values, but that would mean introducing new options, and potentially confusion for the developers using this widget. We've decided that the use cases here are simple ones, and that we should allow the time to be displayed with as few options as possible.

The options we're defining here aren't new; the `step` and `numberFormat` options are already defined by the spinner widget, we're just setting them to default values that make sense for our time widget. The `step` value will be incrementing against a `timestamp` value, and so we give it a default that will step by one second. The `numberFormat` option specifies the format, the spinner expects when parsing, and when formatting output.

Our extension of the spinner, the `_parse()` method, is where we're using the Globalize library directly to parse the time strings. Recall that our inputs have the same string formats. This becomes a problem if we're trying to parse a value that has an unrecognizable format. So we try to parse the time value without specifying what culture the value is. If that doesn't work, we use the culture attached to this widget. This way, we can specify the initial values using one format, as we've done here, and we can change the culture on-the-fly; everything will still work. Our version of the `_format()` method is simple since we know the value is always going to be a timestamp number, all we have to do is pass a new `Date` object back to the original spinner `_format()` method.

Lastly, we have the two time widget instances, where one is passed a culture of `en-CA`, and the other, `en-GB`.

Controlling the step between values

There are several ways with which we can control the steps in the spinner widget. The step is the value that the spinner widget uses to move its number either up or down. For example, you'll often see loop code that increments a counter `cnt ++`. Here, the step is one and this is what the spinner step value defaults to. Changing this option in the spinner is trivial; we can even change this value after the widget has been created.

There are other measures we can take to control the stepping behavior of the spinner. Let's take a look at the incremental option and see how this impacts the spinner.

How to do it...

We'll create three spinner widgets to demonstrate the potential of the incremental option. Following is the HTML structure:

```
<div class="spinner-container">
    <h3>Non-incremental</h3>
    <input id="spin1" />
</div>

<div class="spinner-container">
    <h3>Doubled</h3>
    <input id="spin2" />
</div>

<div class="spinner-container">
    <h3>Faster and Faster</h3>
    <input id="spin3" />
</div>
```

And following is the JavaScript used to create the three spinner instances:

```
$(function() {

    $( "#spin1" ).spinner({
        step: 5,
        incremental: false
    });

    $( "#spin2" ).spinner({
        step: 10,
        incremental: function( spins ) {
            if ( spins >= 10 ) {
                return 2;
            }
            return 1;
        }
    });

    $( "#spin3" ).spinner({
        step: 15,
        incremental: function( spins ) {
            var multiplier = Math.floor( spins / 100 ),
                limit = Math.pow( 10, 10 );
```

```
                if ( multiplier < limit && multiplier > 0 ) {
                    return multiplier;
                }
                return 1;
            }
        });

    });
```

The three spinner widgets should look something like this in your browser.

How it works...

We've created three different spinner instances, all of which behave differently when the user holds down one of the spin buttons. The `#spin1` spinner has a step value of 5, and will always increment the spinner value by 5. You can try this out by holding down the spinner button. You'll notice this will take you a really long time to get to a larger integer value.

The `incremental` option takes a boolean value, as we saw with the first spinner, but it also accepts a `callback` function. The `#spin2` spinner has a step value of 10, but that will change based on our function passed to the incremental option. This `incremental` `callback` function we've defined gets passed through the number of spins that have happened, since the user held the spin button down. We start off normally here, for the first 10 spins, and then we pick up speed from that point forward by returning 2 instead of 1. When we return 2, our step value becomes 20 since the returned value of this function is a multiplier. But it's only used while the user is holding down the spin button; this function doesn't permanently alter the `step` option.

Our last spinner instance, `#spin3`, also uses an `incremental` `callback` function. However, this function will use a progressively larger value as the user continues to spin. Every hundred spins, we increase the multiplier, and also the step. This latter incremental function is useful as the spinner value itself gets larger, and we can control the pace at which the step changes.

There's more...

We've just seen how to control the step of the value of the spinner widget. The `step` option dictates how far, in either direction, the value moves for a given spin. When the user holds the spin button down, we can use the use the `incremental` option to compute a step value. This helps speed up, or slow down the time it takes to spin to a given destination value.

Another approach is to alter the actual timing delay in-between spins. This might be handy, if you want to slow the spinning down, when the user is holding down the spin button. Let's look at an example of how we would go about altering the spin delay. Following is the HTML structure:

```html
<div class="spinner-container">
    <h3>Default delay</h3>
    <input id="spin1" />
</div>

<div class="spinner-container">
    <h3>Long delay</h3>
    <input id="spin2" />
</div>

<div class="spinner-container">
    <h3>Longer delay</h3>
    <input id="spin3" />
</div>
```

And here is the custom spinner widget definition, and three instances that all use different spin values.

```javascript
( function( $, undefined ) {

$.widget( "ab.spinner", $.ui.spinner, {

    options: {
        spinDelay: 40
    },

    _repeat: function( i, steps, event ) {

        var spinDelay = this.options.spinDelay;

        i = i || 500;

        clearTimeout( this.timer );
```

```
            this.timer = this._delay(function() {
                this._repeat( spinDelay, steps, event );
            }, i );

            this._spin( steps * this.options.step, event );

        }

    });

})( jQuery );

$(function() {

    $( "#spin1" ).spinner();

    $( "#spin2" ).spinner({
        spinDelay: 80
    });

    $( "#spin3" ).spinner({
        spinDelay: 120
    });

});
```

You can try each one of these spinners in the browser, and observe the contrast in spin delay.

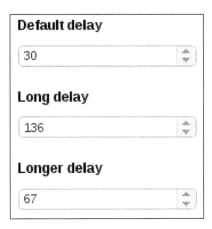

The new `spinDelay` option we've added to the spinner widget allows us to specify the delay in milliseconds. In order to actually use this option, we have to perform some alterations in one of the core spinner widget methods. The `_repeat()` method is used internally by the widget when the user holds down the spinner button. It actually does a fair amount of work using little code. Essentially, the goal is to repeat the given event, over and over, until the user lifts the button and the spinning should stop. However, we cannot just call `_spin()` over and over without some kind of delay, otherwise the user would see nothing more than a blur each time the text input is updated with a new value. And so, the spinner makes use of the `_delay()` method for this exact purpose. The `_delay()` method sets a delayed execution for the past function, and is defined in the `base widget` class; all widgets have access to `_delay()`.

Our version of the `_repeat()` method is nearly identical to the original, except we're not hard-coding the delay between spins; we get that from the `spinDelay` option now.

Specifying the spin overflow

The spinner widget will happily let the user spin, indefinitely. It'll even change the display to use exponential notation when the JavaScript integer limit is reached, that's fine. Almost no application needs to worry about these limits. And in fact, it's probably best to put some limitations in place that actually make sense for the application. That is, specify a `min` boundary and a `max` boundary.

This works well, but it could work even better if we plug some logic into the spinner that handles overflow, when the user wants to go beyond the boundary. Rather than just stop spinning as is the default behavior, we just send them in the same direction, but starting from the opposite boundary. The best way to picture these constraints is by default, the spinner min-max boundary is like a straight line. We want to make it look more like a circle.

How to do it...

We'll have two spinner widgets, the first using the default boundary constraint logic, and the second using our own custom-defined behavior. Following is the HTML structure used to create the two widgets:

```
<div class="spinner-container">
    <h3>Default</h3>
    <input id="spin1" />
</div>

<div class="spinner-container">
    <h3>Overflow</h3>
    <input id="spin2" />
</div>
```

And, here is the JavaScript used to instantiate the two spinners when the document has loaded:

```
$(function() {

    $( "#spin1" ).spinner({
        min: 1,
        max: 100
    });

    $( "#spin2" ).spinner({
        minOverflow: 1,
        maxOverflow: 100,
        spin: function( e, ui ) {

            var value = ui.value,
                minOverflow = $( this ).spinner
                    ( "option", "minOverflow" ),
                    maxOverflow = $( this ).spinner
                        ( "option", "maxOverflow" );

            if ( value > maxOverflow ) {
                $( this ).spinner( "value", minOverflow );
                return false;
            }
            else if ( value < minOverflow ) {
                $( this ).spinner( "value", maxOverflow );
                return false;
            }

        }
    });

});
```

Following are the two widgets in the browser. The latter spinner, you'll see, handles the boundary overflow differently than the default implementation.

How it works...

When the `#spin1` spinner reaches either of the boundaries, 1 or 100, the spinning will just stop. On the other hand, the `#spin2` spinner will pick up at the other end. You'll notice that we're passing two non-standard spinner options here; `minOverflow` and `maxOverflow`. These don't actually constrain the boundary of the spinner the way `min` and `max` do. Adding these new options was intentional on our part because we don't want the regular constraint logic to fire.

The `spin` callback function we've supplied to this widget gets called on every spin. If we had used the traditional spinning `min` and `max` options, we would never know if we're experiencing an overflow because `min` would be less than 1 and `max` would never be more than 100. So, we use the new options to redirect the value, depending on the direction. If the value has gone above 100, then we set the value back to `minOverflow`. Or if the value has gone below 1, then we set the value to `maxOverflow`.

There's more...

You may decide that the overflow behavior, where we bring the user around to the other side of the spinner boundary, it isn't exactly what you're looking for. You may just want to stop the spinning, once the boundary is reached. However, we can still improve on the widget by disabling the spinner button once the boundary in that direction has been reached. This is just a different approach to spinner overflow, whereby we simply supply better feedback to the user, as opposed to altering the business logic as we did earlier. Let's take a look at how we can make this change. Following is the HTML structure used for a simple spinner widget:

```
<div class="spinner-container">
    <input id="spin" value=10 />
</div>
```

And here is our JavaScript used to create the widget once the page loads.

```
$(function() {

    $( "#spin" ).spinner({
        min: 1,
        max: 100,
        spin: function( e, ui ) {
            var value = ui.value,
                buttons = $( this ).data( "uiSpinner" ).buttons,
                min = $( this ).spinner( "option", "min" ),
                max = $( this ).spinner( "option", "max" );
```

```
            if ( value === max ) {
                buttons.filter( ".ui-spinner-up:not
                  (.ui-state-disabled)" )
                        .button( "disable" );
            }
            else if ( value === min ) {
                buttons.filter( ".ui-spinner-down:not
                  (.ui-state-disabled)" )
                        .button( "disable" );
            }
            else {
                buttons.filter( ".ui-state-disabled" )
                .button( "enable" );
            }
        }
    });

});
```

When you start interacting with this widget in the browser, you'll notice that when you hit the min option value, in this case, 1, the down spinner button is disabled.

Likewise, when you hit the max, which is 100 here, the up spinner button is disabled.

We've introduced this new spinner behavior by passing the constructor a spin callback function, executed on each spin. In this callback, we create a reference to both spinner buttons in the buttons variable. Then we check if either the max value has been reached, or if the min value has been reached. We then disable the appropriate button. If we're somewhere in-between min and max, then we simply enable the buttons. You'll also notice that we have some extra filtering involved here; not(.ui-state-disabled) and .ui-state-disabled. This is necessary because of the way the spinner widget fires spin events. Disabling buttons can trigger a spin, leading to an infinite loop. And so we have to take care to disable only those buttons that haven't been disabled yet.

Simplifying the spinner buttons

The default spin buttons implemented in the spinner widget might be a bit much, depending on context. For example, you can clearly see that these are button widgets added to the slider as subcomponents. And this works perfectly when we get to build larger widgets out of smaller ones. This is more along the lines of an aesthetic preference. Maybe the spinner would look better if the individual up and down spin buttons didn't have a hover state, and didn't have a background or border, either for that matter. Let's try taking these style properties away from the buttons in the slider and make them appear more tightly integrated.

How to do it...

Here is the basic HTML structure used as the foundation of our `spinner` widget:

```
<div class="spinner-container">
    <input id="spin" />
</div>
```

And here is the CSS we'll use to remove the button styles we're no longer interested in:

```
.ui-spinner-basic > a.ui-button {
    border: none;
    background: none;
    cursor: pointer;
}
```

The `input` element isn't yet a widget, and the new CSS class we've created isn't yet part of the spinner widget. Here is what the JavaScript code to do both of those things, looks like:

```
(function( $, undefined ) {

$.widget( "ab.spinner", $.ui.spinner, {

    options: {
        basic: false
    },

    _create: function() {

        this._super();

        if ( this.options.basic ) {
            this.uiSpinner.addClass( "ui-spinner-basic" );
        }
```

```
    }

});

})( jQuery );

$(function() {

    $( "#spin" ).spinner({
        basic: true
    });

});
```

If you take a look at the spinner we've created in the browser, you'll notice that the borders and backgrounds of the spinner buttons have been stripped. It now looks more like one whole widget. You'll also notice that the mouse cursor uses a pointer icon when the user hovers over either of the buttons, which helps indicate that they're clickable.

How it works...

The new CSS class we've just created, `ui-spinner-basic`, works by overriding the button widget styles within the context of the spinner. Specifically, we're removing the `border` and `background`, from both the button widgets. In addition, we have set the `cursor` property to `pointer` in order to give the user the impression that the arrows are clickable. We've also customized the definition of the spinner widget itself a little bit. We've done so by adding a new `basic` option, which when `true`, will apply the new `ui-spinner-basic` class to the widget. We don't need to explicitly remove this class when the widget is destroyed because it was added to an element that is created by the spinner widget. This element is automatically removed by the base spinner implementation, and so our code doesn't have to worry about it.

10
Using Tabs

In this chapter, we will cover:

- ▶ Working with remote tab content
- ▶ Giving tabs an icon
- ▶ Simplifying the tab theme
- ▶ Using tabs as URL navigation links
- ▶ Creating effects between tab transitions
- ▶ Sorting tabs using the sortable interaction
- ▶ Setting the active tab using href

Introduction

The **tabs** widget is a container used to organize the content on your page. It is an excellent way to consolidate your page content so only the relevant items are displayed. The user has an easy navigation mechanism to activate content. The tabs widget can be applied in a larger navigational context, where the tabs widget is the main top-level container element for the page. It can also serve well as a smaller component for a specific page element, used to simply split two sections of content.

The tabs widget in the latest jQuery UI version offers the developer a cohesive set of options to tweak the behavior of the widget. We'll look at how we can combine these options, as well as how to get the most out of the navigational pieces of the tabs widget. We'll also explore applying effects to tab transitions, and making tabs sortable for the user.

Working with remote tab content

The tabs widget knows how to populate a given tab panel with remote content out of the box. It's all about how we specify the tab links. For example, an `href` attribute that points to `#tab-content-home` will load the content using the HTML found in that element. But, if instead of pointing to an already-existing element we point to another page, the tabs widget will load the content into the appropriate panel on demand.

This works as expected without passing options to the tabs, but there is the `beforeLoad` option should we want to tweak the behavior of the Ajax request in an any way. Let's take a look at some of the ways we can work with remote content using the tabs widget.

How to do it...

First, we'll create the HTML for our tabs widget, which consists of four links. The first three point to existing resources while the fourth doesn't exist, and so the Ajax request will fail.

```html
<div id="tabs">
    <ul>
        <li><a href="ajax/tab1.html">Tab 1</a></li>
        <li><a href="ajax/tab2.html">Tab 2</a></li>
        <li><a href="ajax/tab3.html">Tab 3</a></li>
        <li><a href="doesnotexist.html">Tab 4</a></li>
    </ul>
</div>
```

Next, we have the JavaScript used to create the tabs widget instance as well as specify some custom behavior to alter the Ajax request.

```javascript
$(function() {

    function tabLoad( e, ui ) {

        if ( ui.panel.html() !== "" ) {

            ui.jqXHR.abort();

        }
        else {

            ui.jqXHR.error(function( data ) {
```

```
        $( "<p/>" ).addClass( "ui-corner-all ui-state-error" )
                .css( "padding", "4px" )
                .text( data.statusText )
                .appendTo( ui.panel );
        });

    }

}

$( "#tabs" ).tabs({
    beforeLoad: tabLoad
});

});
```

In order to view the Ajax behavior implemented in this demonstration, you'll want to put a web server in front of it. The easiest way to do that is to install Python and run `python -m SimpleHTTPServer` from the directory with the main HTML file, as well as the Ajax content files, `tab1.html`, `tab2.html`, and `tab3.html`. Here is an example of what the tab1.html file looks like:

```
<!doctype html>
<html lang="en">
    <body>
        <h1>Tab 1</h1>
        <p>Tab 1 content</p>
    </body>
</html>
```

When you load this tabs widget in your browser, the first tab is selected by default. So the widget will perform the Ajax request that loads the first tab's content right away. You should see something like this:

Switching to the second and third tabs will execute the Ajax request necessary to fetch the content. On the other hand, the fourth tab will result in an error as the linked resource doesn't exist. Instead of content being displayed in that panel, our custom behavior that we've added to the Ajax request displays an error message.

The last thing to note about this example is our other modification to the Ajax request. If you were to revisit the first tab, we're not sending another Ajax request as we already have the panel content.

How it works...

We're creating a tabs widget from the `#tabs` div when the document has finished loading. We're passing `beforeLoad` a callback function, `tabLoad()`, defined earlier. The `tabLoad` function gets called just before the Ajax request to fetch the tab panel content that is dispatched. This gives us an opportunity to update the state of the `jqXHR` object.

The `jqXHR` object returned by `$.ajax()` is an extension of the native `XMLHTTPRequest` type found in JavaScript. Developers seldom interact with this object but occasionally, the need does arise as we've seen here.

The first thing we're checking for in this example is whether or not the tab panel has any content in it. The `ui.panel` object represents the `div` element where the dynamic Ajax content will eventually land. If it is an empty string, we continue loading the content. If, on the other hand, there is content already, we abort the request. This is useful if the server isn't generating dynamic content and we're merely using this feature of the tabs widget as a means of structural composition. There is no point in requesting the same content over and over when we already have it.

We're also attaching behavior to the jqXHR object that's executed if the Ajax request fails. We update the tab content with the status text returned by the server after formatting it using the ui-state-error and ui-corner-all classes.

There's more...

The preceding example took the HTML retrieved from the remote resource and placed it into the tab panel. But now we've decided that the h1 tags in the tab content are redundant, as the active tab serves the same purpose. We can take the tags directly out of the remote resource that we're using to build the tab content, but that could pose a problem if we're using that resource somewhere else in the application. Instead, we can just alter the tab content before the user actually sees it using the load event. Here is a modified version of our tabs widget instance:

```
$(function() {

    function beforeLoad( e, ui ) {

        ui.jqXHR.error(function( data ) {

            ui.panel.empty();

            $( "<p/>" ).addClass( "ui-corner-all ui-state-error" )
                       .css( "padding", "4px" )
                       .text( data.statusText )
                       .appendTo( ui.panel );
        });

    }

    function afterLoad( e, ui ) {
        $( "h1", ui.panel ).remove();
    }

    $( "#tabs" ).tabs({
        beforeLoad: beforeLoad,
        load: afterLoad
    });

});
```

Looking at it now, you'll see that there is no longer a header inside the tab panel. Our `load` callback passed to the tabs in the constructor will find and remove any `h1` tags. The `load` event is triggered after the Ajax call has returned and the content inserted into the panel. We don't need to worry about the `h1` tags appearing after our code has run.

Giving tabs an icon

The tabs widget uses anchor elements, which when clicked, activate the various tab panels to reveal their content. This anchor element only displays text by default, which is good enough under the vast majority of circumstances. There are other times, however, where the tab link itself would benefit from an icon. For example, a house icon helps quickly cue what is in the panel content before actually activating it. Let's look at how we can extend the tab's capabilities to support using both an icon and text as the tab button.

How to do it...

We'll create a basic `tabs` div to support our widget that looks like the following:

```
<div id="tabs">
    <ul>
        <li data-icon="ui-icon-home">
            <a href="#home">Home</a>
        </li>
        <li data-icon="ui-icon-search">
            <a href="#search">Search</a>
        </li>
        <li data-icon="ui-icon-wrench">
            <a href="#settings">Settings</a>
        </li>
    </ul>
    <div id="home">
        <p>Home panel...</p>
    </div>
    <div id="search">
        <p>Search panel...</p>
    </div>
```

```
        <div id="settings">
            <p>Settings panel...</p>
        </div>
    </div>
```

Next, we have our JavaScript, including an extension to the tabs widget that understands how to utilize the new `data-icon` attributes we've included in the markup.

```
(function( $, undefined ) {

$.widget( "ab.tabs", $.ui.tabs, {

    _processTabs: function() {

        this._super();

        var iconTabs = this.tablist.find( "> li[data-icon]" );

        iconTabs.each( function( i, v ) {

            var $tab = $( v ),
                iconClass = $tab.attr( "data-icon" ),
                iconClasses = "ui-icon " +
                            iconClass +
                            " ui-tabs-icon",
                $icon = $( "<span/>" ).addClass( iconClasses ),
                $anchor = $tab.find( "> a.ui-tabs-anchor" ),
                $text = $( "<span/>" ).text( $anchor.text() );

            $anchor.empty()
                    .append( $icon )
                    .append( $text );

        });
    },

    _destroy: function() {

        var iconTabs = this.tablist.find( "> li[data-icon]" );

        iconTabs.each( function( i, v ) {

            var $anchor = $( v ).find( "> a.ui-tabs-anchor" ),
                text = $anchor.find( "> span:not(.ui-icon)" )
                            .text();
```

```
            $anchor.empty().text( text );

        });

        this._super();

    }

  });

})( jQuery );

$(function() {

    $( "#tabs" ).tabs();

});
```

If you were to look at this tabs widget in the browser, you'll notice that each tab button now has an icon to the left of the button text.

How it works...

What's interesting about this customization to the tabs widget is that we're passing the data through the li elements that represent the tab buttons. As any given tabs widget instance could have any number of tabs, it'd be hard to specify which tab gets which icon through the options object. Instead, we're simply transferring these options through the use of a data attribute, data-icon. The value is the icon class we'd like to use from the theme framework.

The changes we've implemented could actually have been done manually in the markup itself, as we're just adding new elements and new classes to the widget. But, there are two problems with this way of thinking. First, there is a lot of manually injected markup that could be generated based on the value of one data attribute—it violates the DRY principle, especially if you're following this pattern for several tabs widgets. Second, we would be introducing new markup that the default widget implementation doesn't know about. It may work out fine, but when things stop working as expected, this can be very difficult to diagnose. And so, we're better off extending the tabs widget.

The `_processTabs()` method we're overriding will iterate over each `li` element that has the `data-icon` attribute, as these are the ones we need to manipulate. The `data-icon` attribute stores the class of icons to use from the theme framework. We construct a `span` element that uses the `ui-icon` class in conjunction with the specific icon class. It also gets our new `ui-tabs-icon` class that properly positions the element inside the link. We're then grabbing the original text of the tab button and wrapping it in a `div`. The reason being, it's easier to insert the icon `span`, followed by the text `span`.

Simplifying the tab theme

Sometimes, the context of our tabs widget has important theme implications. The default visual components of the tabs widget work best when the widget is near the top of the document, that is, the majority of the page content is nested within the tab panels. In contrast, there may be preexisting page elements that could benefit from being organized by a tabs widget. And therein lies the challenge—stuffing a top-level widget such as tabs into a smaller block can look awkward at best, unless we can figure out a way to strip down some unnecessary theme components from the tabs.

How to do it...

Let's first create ourselves some markup to base the tabs widget on. It should look something like the following:

```html
<div id="tabs-container">
    <div id="tabs">
        <ul>
            <li><a href="#tab1">Tab 1</a></li>
            <li><a href="#tab2">Tab 2</a></li>
            <li><a href="#tab3">Tab 3</a></li>
        </ul>
        <div id="tab1">
            <h3>Tab 1...</h3>
            <ul>
                <li>Item 1</li>
                <li>Item 2</li>
                <li>Item 3</li>
            </ul>
        </div>
        <div id="tab2">
            <h3>Tab 2...</h3>
            <ul>
                <li>Item 4</li>
                <li>Item 5</li>
                <li>Item 6</li>
```

```
            </ul>
        </div>
        <div id="tab3">
            <h3>Tab 3...</h3>
            <ul>
                <li>Item 7</li>
                <li>Item 8</li>
                <li>Item 9</li>
            </ul>
        </div>
    </div>
</div>
```

Next, we'll define some CSS used by the tabs widget and the tabs widget container.

```css
div.ui-tabs-basic {
    border: none;
    background: none;
}

div.ui-tabs-basic > ul.ui-tabs-nav {
    background: none;
    border-left: none;
    border-top: none;
    border-right: none;
}

#tabs-container {
    width: 22%;
    background: #f7f7f7;
    padding: 0.9em;
}
```

Next comes our JavaScript code that creates the tabs widget once the document is ready.

```javascript
$(function() {

    $( "#tabs" ).tabs({
        create: function( e, ui ) {
            $( this ).addClass( "ui-tabs-basic" )
                    .find( "> ul.ui-tabs-nav" )
                    .removeClass( "ui-corner-all" );
        }
    });

});
```

How it works...

The `create` function we're passing to the tabs constructor gets triggered after the widget is created. This is where we're adding our custom class, `ui-tabs-basic`, which is used to override the `background` and `border` settings. These are the components we would like to be removed, and so we just set them to `none`. We're also removing the `ui-corner-all` class from the tabs navigation section because we're keeping the bottom border, and leaving this class doesn't look right.

Creating this widget normally, that is, without passing our `create` function, the tabs widget would look something like this:

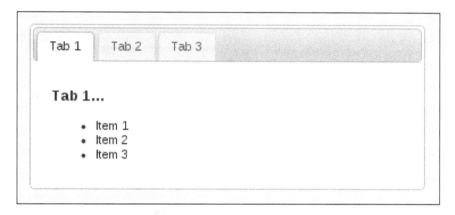

As you can see, it looks like the tabs widget was stuffed into the `#tabs-container` element without much thought. After our simplifications were introduced, the tabs take on a more natural look inside their new context.

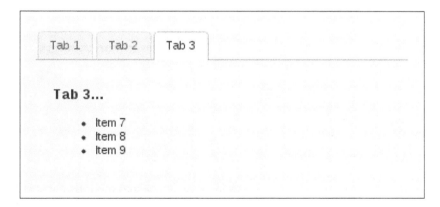

There's more...

If you're using this slimmed-down version of the tabs widget in several places throughout your UI, it can be cumbersome to define a function callback several times to pass to the tabs constructor. You could define the callback function once and pass a reference to it in the constructor, but then you still have the callback function out in the open. From a design perspective, we might want to encapsulate this behavior in the tabs widget and expose it to the outside world through a widget option. Here is a modification of the example that does just that:

```
(function( $, undefined ) {

$.widget( "ab.tabs", $.ui.tabs, {

    options: {
        basic: false
    },

    _create: function() {

        this._super();

        if ( !this.options.basic ) {
            return;
        }

        $( this.element ).addClass( "ui-tabs-basic" )
                         .find( "> ul.ui-tabs-nav" )
                         .removeClass( "ui-corner-all" );

    }

});

})( jQuery );

$(function() {

    $( "#tabs" ).tabs({
        basic: true
    });

});
```

Here, we've moved the functionality previously in our callback into the tabs constructor, but it's only ever executed if the `basic` option is set to `true`, and it defaults to `false`.

Using tabs as URL navigation links

The tabs widget isn't limited to populating tab panels using preloaded div elements or by making Ajax calls. Some applications already have many components built, and lots of content to display. If you're updating a site, or application such as this, the tabs widget might be useful as the main form of navigation, especially if you're already using jQuery UI widgets. What we would need then is something generic that could be applied to every page, without much effort on the part of the developer using the widget. Although the tabs widget wasn't designed for such a purpose, we're not going to let that stop us because with a little tweaking, we can create a generic component that gives us exactly what we need.

How to do it...

The first thing we'll look at is the content on one of the pages in our application. The HTML defines both the tabs widget structure and the content displayed under the active tab.

```html
<div id="nav">
    <ul>
        <li>
            <a href="tab1.html">Tab 1</a>
        </li>
        <li>
            <a href="tab2.html">Tab 2</a>
        </li>
        <li>
            <a href="tab3.html">Tab 3</a>
        </li>
    </ul>
    <div>
        <p>Tab 1 content...</p>
    </div>
</div>
```

You'll notice that there are three pages in this application, and they each use the same widget HTML structure; the only difference is the tab content paragraph. Next, we'll define our new navigation widget and create it on the page. This same JavaScript code is included on each page of the application.

```javascript
(function( $, undefined ) {

$.widget( "ab.nav", $.ui.tabs, {

    _initialActive: function() {

        var path = location.pathname,
            path = path.substring( path.search( /[^\/]+$/ ) ),
```

```
                    tabs = this.tabs,
                    $active = tabs.find( "> a[href$='" + path + "']" );

            return tabs.find( "a" )
                        .index( $active );
        },

        _eventHandler: function( event ) {

            window.open( $( event.target ).attr( "href" ), "_self" );

        },

        _createPanel: function( id ) {

            var panel = this.element.find( "> div:first" );

            if ( !panel.hasClass( "ui-tabs-panel" ) ) {
                panel.data( "ui-tabs-destroy", true )
                    .addClass( "ui-tabs-panel " +
                                "ui-widget-content " +
                                "ui-corner-bottom" );

            }

            return panel;

        },

        _getPanelForTab: function( tab ) {

            return this.element.find( "> div:first" );

        },

        load: $.noop

    });

})( jQuery );

$(function() {

    $( "#nav" ).nav();

});
```

Now, when you interact with this navigation widget, you'll see that each time you activate a new tab, the browser will reload the page to point at the tab's `href`; for example, `tab3.html`.

How it works...

Let's first look at the HTML structure before we discuss the new `nav` widget we've created. The first thing to note is that the HTML structure we've provided here is different from what the tabs widget is expecting. We have a `div` element that holds the main content of the page and it has no ID, and thus no way for any tab link to reference it. Not to worry though, this is intentional. The `nav` widget is designed for sites or applications that have multiple pages—we're not embedding multiple tab pane content in this widget. With this structural change to the HTML the widget uses, it's best that we create an entirely new widget rather than just extend the tabs widget. This approach will avoid confusion as to what the HTML structure of a tabs widget should look like.

The goal of our `nav` widget, based on the tabs widget, is to activate the appropriate tab and render the `div` element as the selected tab panel. When a tab link is clicked, we don't perform any of the usual tab activities, we simply follow `href`.

All the methods we're overriding in the definition of the `nav` widget come from the tabs widget, and for the most part, we're replacing the tabs functionality we don't need. The first method is `_initialActive()`, which determines the active tab when the widget is first created. Here, we're basing this decision on the path in the location object. We compare it to the tab's `href` attributes. Next is the `_eventHandler()` method. This method gets called when the user activates a tab. Here, we're just performing the same action as a default browser link and following the `href` attribute of the tab link. As we're doing this in the `_eventHandler()` method, the `keypress` events used to switch tabs will still work as expected. Next, the `_createPanel()` method is called when the tabs widget needs to create and insert a tab panel. The reason the tabs widget calls this method is that it needs a panel when making Ajax calls. As we're not making any Ajax calls in our `nav` widget, this method will now use the default `div` that has the content of the page. The only changes we're making to the content `div` is adding the appropriate tab panel CSS classes. Finally, we have the `_getPanelForTab()` method that returns our content `div`, the only one that matters for this widget, and the `load()` method is `$.noop`. This prevents the widget from trying to load Ajax content when the widget is first created.

Creating effects between tab transitions

The tabs widget lets the developer specify an effect to run when transitioning between tabs. Specifically, we're able to tell the tabs widget to run a specific effect when showing a tab, and another effect when hiding a tab. When the user clicks on a tab, both of these effects, if specified, are run. First the hide effect, followed by the show effect. Let's take a look at how we can combine these two tabs options to enhance the interactivity of the widget.

How to do it...

First, we'll create the necessary HTML structure we need to build our tabs widget. It should look something along the lines of what follows, producing three tabs:

```html
<div id="tabs">
    <ul>
        <li><a href="#tab1">Tab 1</a></li>
        <li><a href="#tab2">Tab 2</a></li>
        <li><a href="#tab3">Tab 3</a></li>
    </ul>
    <div id="tab1">
        <p>Tab 1 content...</p>
        <button>Tab 1 Button</button>
    </div>
    <div id="tab2">
        <p>Tab 2 content...</p>
        <strong>Tab 2 bold text</strong>
    </div>
    <div id="tab3">
        <p>Tab 3 content...</p>
        <p>...and more content</p>
    </div>
</div>
```

Next, the following JavaScript code instantiates the tabs widget, with the `show` and `hide` effect options passed to the widget constructor.

```javascript
$(function() {

    $( "#tabs" ).tabs({
        show: {
            effect: "slide",
            direction: "left"
        },
        hide: {
```

```
            effect: "drop",
            direction: "right"
        }
    });

});
```

How it works...

When you view this tabs widget in your browser and click through the tabs, you'll notice how the content of the current tab slides to the right, while fading out at the same time. Once this effect has finished execution, the `show` effect of the now-active tab runs, and in this case, slides the content in from the left. The two effects complement each other—when combined, they create an illusion of the new content pushing the old out of the panel.

The two effects we've chosen here are actually very similar. The `drop` effect is really just the `slide` effect with the addition of fading while sliding. The key to their collaboration is the `direction` property we've passed to each `effect` object. We've told the `hide` effect to move to the right when it runs. Likewise, we've told the `show` effect to enter from the left.

Sorting tabs using the sortable interaction

When we implement tabs in a user interface, we might briefly consider the default ordering of the tabs. Obviously, we want the most relevant tabs accessible to the user in an order that makes most sense to them. But we seldom get this right in a way that makes everyone happy. So why not let the user arrange the tabs in a way that they see fit? Let's see if we can recruit the sortable interaction widget for some help by providing this capability in the tabs widget.

How to do it...

We'll use the following as the sample HTML driving our tabs instance:

```
<div id="tabs">
    <ul>
        <li><a href="#tab1">Tab 1</a></li>
        <li><a href="#tab2">Tab 2</a></li>
        <li><a href="#tab3">Tab 3</a></li>
    </ul>
    <div id="tab1">
        <p>Tab 1 content...</p>
    </div>
    <div id="tab2">
        <p>Tab 2 content...</p>
```

```
        </div>
        <div id="tab3">
            <p>Tab 3 content...</p>
        </div>
    </div>
```

Next, we'll implement the new `sortable` option in the tabs widget. We'll also need to extend the widget's behavior to take advantage of this new option.

```
(function( $, undefined ) {

$.widget( "ab.tabs", $.ui.tabs, {

    options: {
        sortable: false
    },

    _create: function() {

        this._super();

        if ( !this.options.sortable ) {
            return;
        }

        this.tablist.sortable({
            axis: "x",
            stop: $.proxy( this, "_stopped" )
        });

    },

    _destroy: function() {

        if ( this.options.sortable ) {
            this.tablist.sortable( "destroy" );
        }

        this._super();

    },

    _stopped: function( e, ui ) {
        this.refresh();
    }

});
```

```
})( jQuery );

$(function() {

    $( "#tabs" ).tabs({
        sortable: true
    });

});
```

Now when you drag the tab buttons along the x axis, dropping them will rearrange their order. For example, dragging the first tab would look something like this:

If we dropped the first tab at the end and activated **Tab 2**, now the first tab, you should see something like this:

How it works...

We've added a new option to the tabs widget, `sortable`, which when true will use the sortable interaction widget to enable the sortable behavior with the tab buttons. We've added this option by setting the default `sortable` value to `false` in the `options` object. This object will be merged with the default tabs options. In the `_create()` method, the tabs constructor, we call the original tabs widget constructor as nothing special needs to happen with the default widget construction. Next, still inside `_create()`, we check that the `sortable` option is `true`, and if so create the sortable widget. The `tablist` property we're using to create the sortable widget with is the `ul` element that holds our tabs buttons. This is why we're calling it here, we want its children to be sortable along the x axis.

We're also passing the `stop` option of the sortable widget a callback function, in this case, a proxy of the `_stopped()` method. This is using the `$.proxy()` utility so that we can implement `_stopped()` as though it is a regular method of tabs. Notice in the `_stopped()` implementation that this is the widget instance, whereas without a proxy, this would be the `ul` element.

Finally, the `_destroy()` method is overridden here to ensure that the sortable widget is destroyed. Without doing so, we couldn't reliably destroy and recreate the tabs widget.

There's more...

We can further enhance the user interaction of the tabs widget when the `sortable` option is set to `true`. First, let's modify `cursor` while the user is dragging the tab so that it uses a standard move icon. Next, we'll activate the dropped tab. Here is the CSS we'll need for the modified cursor; we'll keep the previous HTML structure as is:

```css
.ui-tabs .ui-tabs-nav li.ui-tab-move > a {
    cursor: move;
}
```

And here is the modified JavaScript:

```javascript
(function( $, undefined ) {

$.widget( "ab.tabs", $.ui.tabs, {

    options: {
        sortable: false
    },

    _create: function() {

        this._super();

        if ( !this.options.sortable ) {
            return;
        }

        this.tablist.sortable({
            axis: "x",
            start: $.proxy( this, "_started" ),
```

```
                stop: $.proxy( this, "_stopped" )
            });

    },

    _destroy: function() {

        if ( this.options.sortable ) {
            this.tablist.sortable( "destroy" );
        }

        this._super();

    },

    _started: function( e, ui ) {
        ui.item.addClass( "ui-tab-move" );
    },

    _stopped: function( e, ui ) {

        ui.item.removeClass( "ui-tab-move" );
        this.refresh();
        this._activate( ui.item.index() );

    }

});

})( jQuery );

$(function() {

    $( "#tabs" ).tabs({
        sortable: true
    });

});
```

Now when you sort these tabs, you'll notice the new cursor is illustrated in the following screenshot. The `ui-tab-move` class defines the `cursor` CSS property, and this class is added to the `li` element in the `start` event handler of the sortable widget. It is subsequently removed in the `stop` handler. You'll also notice that the tab is activated when the tab is dropped. This is done by getting the index of the `li` element and passing that to the `activate()` method.

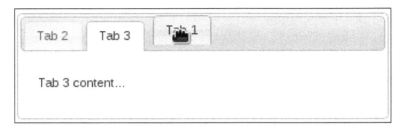

Setting the active tab using href

The tabs widget allows the developer to programmatically set the active tab. This can be done by passing a zero-based index value to the `active` option. This option can be set in the tabs constructor, which tells the widget which tab to activate by default, or it can be set afterwards, potentially changing the active tab. Changing the active tab using this option is essentially the same thing as a user clicking on a tab button to activate the panel. However, we can improve on this interface by allowing developers using the tabs widget to pass an `href` value instead of an index. This way, you don't have to remember the ordering of the tabs—which number represents which link, and so on.

How to do it...

Let's first set up the HTML used in this demonstration as the foundation of the tabs widget.

```
<div id="tabs">
    <ul>
        <li><a href="#tab1">Tab 1</a></li>
        <li><a href="#tab2">Tab 2</a></li>
        <li><a href="#tab3">Tab 3</a></li>
    </ul>
    <div id="tab1">
        <p>Tab 1 content...<a class="tab-link" href="#tab2">tab 2</
a></p>
    </div>
    <div id="tab2">
        <p>Tab 2 content...<a class="tab-link" href="#tab3">tab 3</
a></p>
```

```
        </div>
        <div id="tab3">
            <p>Tab 3 content...<a class="tab-link" href="#tab1">tab 1</
a></p>
        </div>
    </div>
```

Next is the modified implementation of the tabs widget that enables us to activate the second tab by passing the string "#tab2" to the active option.

```
(function( $, undefined ) {

$.widget( "ab.tabs", $.ui.tabs, {

    _findActive: function( index ) {
        return this._super( this._getIndex( index ) );
    },

    _initialActive: function() {

        this.options.active = this._getIndex( this.options.active );
        return this._super();

    }

});

})( jQuery );

$(function() {

    $( "#tabs" ).tabs({
        active: "#tab2"
    });

    $( ".tab-link" ).on( "click", function( e ) {
        e.preventDefault();
        $( "#tabs" ).tabs( "option", "active", $( this ).attr( "href"
) );
    });

});
```

How it works...

You'll notice that when you look at this tabs widget in the browser, the second tab is activated by default as we're passing in the string `"#tab2"`. You'll also notice that the content of each tab panel has a link pointing to another tab.

We're extending the tabs widget so that we can override a couple of tabs methods. The first method is `_findActive()`, which in the original implementation expects an integer. We've changed this to use the `_getIndex()` method that returns the index based on the `href` attribute of the tab button, that is, unless it gets an integer value passed to it, in which case, it just returns that number. In short, we've changed `_findActive()` to accept either a zero-based index number, or an `href` string.

The next method is `_initialActive()`, which is called when the tabs widget is first instantiated. What we're doing here is setting the active option to the appropriate index value before calling the original implementation of `_initialActive()`. This is necessary to support the `href` string in the constructor as the `active` option value.

Finally, we're creating our tabs widget using an `href` string, and we're binding an event handler to each of the tab-link anchors in the tab panels. Here, we're activating the tab based solely on the `href` attribute of the link, so you can see the value of this new `href` capability we've introduced.

There's more...

In the preceding example, we're utilizing the `href` attribute of the tab button links. However, we're not utilizing the location hash of the browser. In other words, when a tab is activated, the location hash in the browser URL doesn't change. There are several advantages to supporting this approach. For one thing, we can use the Back button to navigate through our active tabs. Another benefit is that our links in the tab content panels no longer need an event handler; they can just point their `href` attributes to the tab `href`.

Here is the modified JavaScript that supports the same functionality as the previous example. The only difference is that the URL hash will change any time a tab is activated.

```
(function( $, undefined ) {

$.widget( "ab.tabs", $.ui.tabs, {

    _create: function() {

        this._super();

        this._on( window, {
            hashchange: $.proxy( this, "_hashChange" )
        });

    },

    _hashChange: function( e ) {

        if ( this.active.attr( "href" ) === location.hash ) {
            return;
        }

        this._activate( this._getIndex( location.hash ) );

    },

    _eventHandler: function( e ) {

        this._super( e );

        var href = $( e.target ).attr( "href" );

        if ( href === location.hash ) {
            return;
        }

        if ( href.indexOf( "#" ) === 0 ) {
            location.hash = href;
        }
        else {
            location.hash = "";
        }

    }
```

```
    });

    })( jQuery );

    $(function() {
        $( "#tabs" ).tabs();
    });
```

Now when you interact with this tabs widget in the browser, you'll notice that the hash changes in the URL as you navigate through the tabs. This is done by adding an event handler to the _create() method, after calling the original implementation of _create(). We're using the _on() utility method to subscribe to the window's hashchange event. Next, the _hashChange() method we've added is the handler for this event. First, we check if the URL hash, stored in the location.hash variable, is already pointing to the active tab. If not, we activate the tab based on the current URL hash value. This is all we need to support the links in the tab panel content that point directly to a URL hash. But, when the user clicks directly on the tab button, there is no change in the hash value. This doesn't help us much because we cannot track the tab navigation history.

This is why we've implemented a customization of the _eventHandler() method. We first call the original implementation of the method before we go about handling the URL hash specifics. If the URL hash is already pointing to the active tab, we have nothing to do here; otherwise, we update the URL hash.

11
Using Tooltips

In this chapter, we will cover:

- ▸ Changing the tooltip state
- ▸ Using custom markup in tooltips
- ▸ Displaying mouse movement
- ▸ Applying effects to the tooltip display
- ▸ Tooltips for selected text

Introduction

In this chapter, we'll explore the various dimensions of the **tooltip** widget, used to provide contextual information to the user. The tooltip widget works well with existing code because by default, it uses standard HTML attributes for the text of the tooltip. Furthermore, it's easy to create tooltip instances for the entire user interface with one line of code.

Going beyond the simple use cases, we'll look at the different types of content we can pass into the widget, and how the content can be generated dynamically. We'll also look at how the tooltip can aid the development process as a tool, and how developers can manipulate the available effects for showing and hiding the widget.

Changing the tooltip state

The visual display of the tooltip widget has a default state. That is, out of the box, the widget is nicely designed, using elements from the theme framework. We may want to change that, however, depending on the state of some resource in the application. For example, a button that is new to the user as a result of a change in permissions might want a tooltip state that stands out visually, relative to the other tooltips on the page. By the same token, if there is a broken resource, and the user hovers over one of its components, the tooltip displayed should take on an error state. Of course, when changing the state of the tooltip, we should keep in mind that the state should match the context and tone of the actual tooltip. For example, don't put an error state on a tooltip that reads "everything is good to go!". Let's look at a quick and easy entry point into tooltip customization. We'll use a standard tooltip option to pass the state CSS class in.

How to do it...

We'll use the following HTML for our tooltip widgets. What we have here are three buttons, each with their own states, and their own tooltip instances.

```
<div class="button-container">
    <button class="tt-default" title="I'm using the default tooltip
state">Default</button>
</div>
<div class="button-container">
    <button class="tt-highlight" title="I'm using the highlight
tooltip state">Highlight</button>
</div>
<div class="button-container">
    <button class="tt-error" title="I'm using the error tooltip
state">Error</button>
</div>
```

Next, we'll create the tooltip widgets for their respective buttons using the following JavaScript:

```
$(function() {

    $( "button" ).tooltip();

    $( "button.tt-highlight" ).tooltip( "option", {
        tooltipClass: "ui-state-highlight"
    });

    $( "button.tt-error" ).tooltip( "option", {
        tooltipClass: "ui-state-error"
    });

});
```

Hovering over each one of the buttons in the browser shows you the default, highlight, and error states as shown in the following images:

▶ The default state:

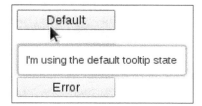

▶ The highlight state:

▶ The error state:

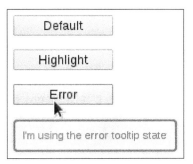

How it works...

For this particular example, we're utilizing the `tooltipClass` option to pass the state CSS classes from the theme framework to the widget. First, we simply make each button on the page a tooltip widget. After this call the tooltip constructor, we have three tooltip instances, all using the default state. Next, we find the button with the `tt-highlight` class and pass the `tooltipClass` option a value of `ui-state-highlight`. Finally, we locate the button with the `tt-error` class and assign that tooltip widget the `ui-state-error` class using the `tooltipClass` option.

There's more...

There are a few downsides to the approach we've used previously. For one thing, the user can't tell that something is wrong till they move their mouse over the element and see that the tooltip is in an error state. In a more realistic scenario, if there were something wrong with the button, it would probably have an error state applied to the button itself. So to apply the error state, we had to invent our own class names and determine at tooltip-creation time which class to use.

A more robust solution would center around using the actual states from the framework on the element instead of inventing our own. Furthermore, the tooltip should be intelligent enough to change its class depending on the state of the element to which it is applied. In other words, if the button has the `ui-state-error` class applied to it, it should use this class as the `tooltipClass` option. Let's add an `inheritState` option to the tooltip widget that'll turn on this behavior.

Here is the modified HTML source:

```
<div class="button-container">
    <button title="I'm using the default tooltip state">Default</
button>
</div>
<div class="button-container">
    <button class="ui-state-highlight" title="I'm using the highlight
tooltip state">Highlight</button>
</div>
<div class="button-container">
    <button class="ui-state-error" title="I'm using the error tooltip
state">Error</button>
</div>
```

And here is the definition of the tooltip widget extension with the new option included:

```
(function( $, undefined ) {

$.widget( "ab.tooltip", $.ui.tooltip, {

    options: {
        inheritState: false
    },

    _create: function() {

        var self = this,
            options = this.options,
            states = [
```

```
                    "ui-state-highlight",
                    "ui-state-error"
            ];

        if ( !options.inheritState || options.tooltipClass ) {
            return this._super();
        }

        $.each( states, function( i, v ) {

            if ( self.element.hasClass( v ) ) {
                self.options.tooltipClass = v;
            }

        });

        this._super();

    }

});

})( jQuery );

$(function() {

    $( "button" ).tooltip({
        inheritState: true
    });

});
```

This version of the code should behave identically to the first iteration. The difference, of course, is that the buttons themselves have a visible state, and we want the tooltip widgets to pick up on that. We tell it to do so by setting the inheritState option to true.

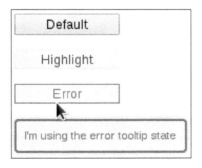

Our new option, `inheritState`, gets added to the default `options` object set forth by the original implementation of the tooltip widget. In the `_create()` method, the widget constructor, we're checking if the `inheritState` option is `true`, or if the `tooltipClass` option has already been set. In either case, we return, calling the original implementation. Otherwise, we check if the element has either of the states in the `states` array, and if so, we set that class as the `tooltipClass`.

Using custom markup in tooltips

We're not limited to using the `title` attribute to supply basic text strings to the tooltip content. Sometimes, the content of the tooltip widget warrants formatting. For example, a title section would have different font styles than that of the main text section. The tooltip widget allows developers to pass in custom content through the `content` option. This can either be a raw string, or a function that returns the content we would like displayed. Let's look at how to go about using this option in your application.

How to do it...

We'll create two `button` elements; each have a `title` attribute, the text of which we'll use in the tooltip. We're also going to add the name of the button as the tooltip title.

```
<div class="button-container">
    <button title="Logs the user in by establishing a new
session.">Login</button>
</div>
<div class="button-container">
    <button title="Deactivates the session, and logs the user
out.">Logout</button>
</div>
```

Next, let's create the basic CSS styles that format our tooltip.

```
.ui-tooltip-title {
    font-weight: bold;
    font-size: 1.1em;
    margin-bottom: 5px;
}
```

Finally, we'll create the tooltip widgets using a custom content function to format the tooltip content.

```
$(function() {

    $( "button" ).tooltip({
        content: function() {
```

```
        var $content = $( "<div/>" );

        $( "<div/>" ).text( $( this ).text() )
                     .addClass( "ui-tooltip-title" )
                     .appendTo( $content );

        $( "<span/>" ).text( $( this ).attr( "title" ) )
                      .appendTo( $content );

        return $content;

    }

  });

});
```

The tooltip, when we hover over one of the `button` elements, should look something like the following screenshot. Notice the formatted title section.

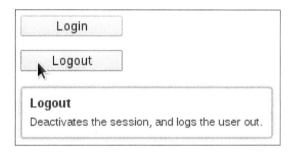

How it works...

The `content` function we've passed to each tooltip widget wraps the content into a `div` element, stored in the `$content` variable. The purpose is to store the title and the main text elements inside this `div`, and that way we simply return the `$content` variable from the function. The title `div` uses the button text, or, its name. This `div` gets the `ui-tooltip-title` class we defined earlier, which simply modifies the font, and adds some space to the bottom of the element. Next, we add the main content `span` element, which just uses the `title` attribute of the element.

There's more...

The approach to modifying the tooltip we've just examined is free-form—the function can return just about anything it wants. Let's look at a more structured approach to modifying the tooltip content. We'll alter the tooltip widget so that it accepts specific content section options. To demonstrate this, we'll utilize the **Rotten Tomatoes API**. The only HTML we'll need is a simple `div` element that looks like `<div class="titles"></div>`. Now let's define the CSS styles for the titles that we're going to list, as well as the specific tooltip content sections.

```css
.titles {
    margin: 20px;
}

.titles img {
    padding: 10px;
}

.ui-tooltip-header {
    font-weight: bold;
    font-size: 1.4em;
}

.ui-tooltip-body {
    margin: 7px 0 7px 0;
    font-size: 1.2em;
}

.ui-tooltip-footer {
    font-weight: bold;
    border-top: solid 1px;
    padding-top: 7px;
}
```

Here is the customized tooltip widget declaration which adds the new content options. When the document loads, we call the Rotten Tomatoes API and display five images in our container `div`. Each image is also a tooltip that uses the new specific content options we've added to the widget.

```javascript
(function( $, undefined ) {

$.widget( "ab.tooltip", $.ui.tooltip, {

    options: {
        header: null,
```

```
        body: null,
        footer: null
},

_create: function() {

    this._super();

    var header = this.options.header,
        body = this.options.body,
        footer = this.options.footer;

    if ( !header && !body && !footer ) {
        return;
    }

    this.options.content = $.proxy( this, "_content" );

},

_content: function() {

    var header = this.options.header,
        body = this.options.body,
        footer = this.options.footer,
        $content = $( "<div/>" );

    if ( header ) {

        $( "<div/>" ).text( header )
                    .addClass( "ui-tooltip-header" )
                    .appendTo( $content );

    }

    if ( body ) {

        $( "<div/>" ).text( body )
                    .addClass( "ui-tooltip-body" )
                    .appendTo( $content );

    }
```

```
                  if ( footer ) {

                      $( "<div/>" ).text( footer )
                                  .addClass( "ui-tooltip-footer" )
                                  .appendTo( $content );

                  }

                  return $content;

              }

          });

      })( jQuery );

      $(function() {

          var apikey = "2vnk...",  // Your Rotten Tomatoes API key goes here
              apibase = "http://api.rottentomatoes.com/api/public/v1.0";

          $.ajax({
              url: apibase + "/lists/movies/in_theaters.json",
              dataType: "jsonp",
              data: {
                  apikey: apikey,
                  page_limit: "5",
              },
              success: function( data ) {

                  $.each( data.movies, function( i, v ) {

                      var $logo = $( "<img/>" );

                      $logo.attr( "src", v.posters.thumbnail )
                          .appendTo( ".titles" );

                      $logo.tooltip({
                          header: v.title,
                          body: v.synopsis.substring( 0, 150 ) + "...",
                          footer: v.year + " (" + v.mpaa_rating + ")",
                          items: "img"
                      });
```

```
        });

    }

  });

});
```

Viewing this page in the browser should populate the titles `div` with five images, and when you hover the mouse pointer over each one, you should see our custom tooltip content.

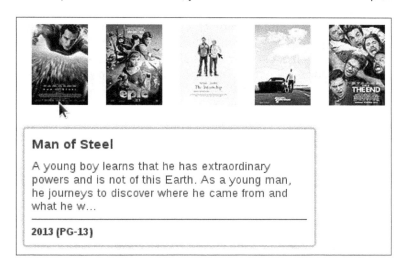

Let's start by looking at the API call we're making to the Rotten Tomatoes API when the document has finished loading. All we're fetching are the first five movies from the in-theaters catalog. We're then creating an `img` element and setting the `src` attribute to the appropriate thumbnail for the movie. This is how the images you see in the example are rendered. We're also calling the tooltip constructor on each of the images, passing to it the new options we've defined. Namely, these are the sections of the tooltip content, the `header`, `body`, and `footer`. Notice, that we have to tell the tooltip that that this is an `img` element and it won't find the tooltip content in the usual places—this is done using the `items` option.

Looking now at our customizations implemented in the tooltip widget, we can see that the options are defined by assigning a new option to the `options` attribute—these get merged into the default tooltip `options` object. Next, we have a custom implementation of the `_create()` method, which is called when the tooltip is instantiated. The goal here is to check if any one of the three content sections has been specified, and if not, we have nothing to do and simply exit. The original version of the `_create()` method was called using `_super()`, and so at this point, the widget has already been created. Our last job in the constructor is to assign the `content` option a function that generates the tooltip content. In this case, it is a proxy to the `_content()` method.

The `_content()` method wraps it's returned HTML in a `div` element, this is stored in the `$content` variable. We then add the specified content to the `div` element as specified in the options. Each content section is a `div` element, and they're given a corresponding CSS class to control the appearance—`ui-tooltip-header`, `ui-tooltip-body`, and `ui-tooltip-footer`.

Displaying the mouse movement

We can use the tooltip widget as an aid during development, and not necessarily a widget that ships with the finished product. For example, we can use the tooltip widget to track the mouse movements and to display the X and Y coordinates. This could help us diagnose some tricky mouse behavior as we're piecing together the UI components. We'll look at tracking the mouse coordinates for specific elements, but bear in mind, the concept is what counts. We can use this technique to display any number of event properties—we simply discard the call when no longer needed.

How to do it...

We'll create the required CSS first. These simply position the `div` elements that we'll want to track mouse movements on.

```
.mouse-tracker {
    margin: 20px;
    background-image: none;
    padding: 3px;
}

.mouse-tracker p {
    font-size: 1.2em;
}

.mouse-tracker-page {
    width: 180px;
    height: 170px;
}

.mouse-tracker-relative {
    width: 150px;
    height: 140px;
}
```

Next comes the HTML itself, two `div` elements that we're in the midst of designing. We'd like our mouse tracking utility to show us what happens when the user moves the mouse over these elements.

```
<div class="ui-widget-content mouse-tracker mouse-tracker-page">
    <p>Page mouse movement</p>
</div>
<div class="ui-widget-content ui-state-default mouse-tracker mouse-
tracker-relative">
    <p>Element mouse movement</p>
</div>
```

Last but not least, we'll implement our tracker tool. It's a widget called tracker and it extends the tooltip widget. We're calling it something else so as to not confuse it with the existing tooltip widget that we're probably using in our production systems.

```
(function( $, undefined ) {

$.widget( "ab.tracker", $.ui.tooltip, {

    options: {
        track: true,
        items: ".ui-tracker",
        relative: false
    },

    _create: function() {

        this.element.addClass( "ui-tracker" );

        this._super();

        this.options.content = $.proxy( this, "_content" );

    },

    _content: function() {

        var $content = $( "<div/>" ),
            relative = this.options.relative,
            xlabel = relative ? "Element X: " : "Page X: ",
            ylabel = relative ? "Element Y: " : "Page Y: ";

        $( "<div/>" ).append( $( "<strong/>" ).text( xlabel ) )
                     .append( $( "<span/>" ).attr( "id", "ui-
tracker-x" ) )
                     .appendTo( $content );

        $( "<div/>" ).append( $( "<strong/>" ).text( ylabel ) )
```

```
                          .append( $( "<span/>" ).attr( "id", "ui-
tracker-y" ) )
                          .appendTo( $content );

        return $content;

    },

    _mousemove: function( e ) {

        var $target = $( e.target ).closest( this.options.items ),
            offset,
            offsetLeft = 0
            offsetTop = 0;

        if ( this.options.relative ) {
            offset = $target.offset();
            offsetLeft = offset.left;
            offsetTop = offset.top;
        }

        $( "#ui-tracker-x" ).text( e.pageX - offsetLeft );
        $( "#ui-tracker-y" ).text( e.pageY - offsetTop );

    },

    open: function( e ) {

        this._super( e );

        var $target = $( e.target ).closest( this.options.items );

        this._on( $target, {
            mousemove: $.proxy( this, "_mousemove" )
        });

    }

});

})( jQuery );

$(function() {
```

```
$( ".mouse-tracker-page" ).tracker();
$( ".mouse-tracker-relative" ).tracker({
    relative: true
});

});
```

Looking at these two `div` elements in the browser, you should see something similar to the following:

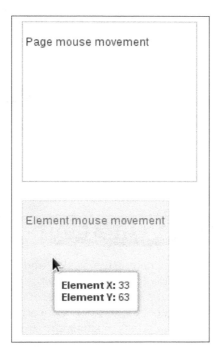

The tracker widget we've just defined extends the tooltip widget by filling in a couple of options with new defaults as well as by providing a new option. The `track` tooltip option tells the widget to position itself relative to the mouse movement. Since we're implementing a mouse coordinate tracker, it makes sense to turn this on by default. The next tooltip option value we want changed is the `items` option. This tells the tooltip which target elements make valid tooltips, and in our case, we would like it to be the class given to our tracker widget—`ui-tracker`. The `relative` option is something new we're adding to the widget. This tells the tracker, when `true`, to display the coordinates relative to the element in question, instead of relative to the page, which is the default.

Next, we're extending the `_create()` method of the tooltip widget, which is the constructor. The first thing we do before calling the original implementation of the constructor is add the track widget class to the element. This is necessary in order for the element to be considered a valid tracker— see the `items` option. Once we've finished with the `_super()` method, we assign the `content` option a callback, which is a proxy to the `_callback()` method of this widget. The `_callback()` method simply returns the template content we want displayed in the tooltip. This includes the X and Y coordinates of the mouse event. We have to figure out if the label should be a page, or if it should be an element, based on the `relative` option.

We're overriding the `open()` method to set up our `mousemove` event handling. Typically, this would be done in the `_create()` method. But there is no need to track the mouse movement when the tooltip isn't open and the callbacks firing would be a waste of valuable CPU cycles. We use the `_on()` utility method to bind a proxy handler to the `_mousemove()` method of this widget. The `_mousemove()` method is responsible for updating the content of the tooltip. Specifically, it sets the text value of the `#ui-tracker-x` and `#ui-tracker-y` labels generated by our `_content()` method. The values of the X and Y coordinates will be based either on the `pageX` and `pageX` properties of the event alone, or in conjunction with the offset values, depending on the `relative` option.

The tracker widget is instantiated in the same way as the tooltip widget. When we no longer need these values displayed, as in, when we're ready to go live, these widget calls would be removed.

Applying effects to the tooltip display

The tooltip widget ships with options to control the display, and hide the actions of the element. These are the `show` and `hide` options, respectfully, and each accepts an object that specifies animation options. Since the `show` and `hide` options control different aspects of the widget display, we have the freedom to use different settings, such as delay for the show and hide actions. Or, we could be drastic about it and use two completely different effects for the animations. Let's explore the various `show` and `hide` options available to us in the tooltip widget.

How to do it...

First, let's create some button elements that we'll use to display the tooltips.

```
<div class="button-container">
    <button class="drop" title="I'm using the drop effect">Drop</
button>
</div>
<div class="button-container">
    <button class="slide" title="I'm using the slide effect">Slide</
button>
</div>
```

```
<div class="button-container">
    <button class="explode" title="I'm using the clip/explode
effect">Explode</button>
</div>
```

Next, we'll instantiate a tooltip widget for each of the buttons, passing in our custom `show` and `hide` animation options.

```
$(function() {

    $( "button" ).tooltip();

    $( "button.drop" ).tooltip( "option", {
        show: {
            effect: "drop",
            delay: 150,
            duration: 450,
            direction: "up",
        },
        hide: {
            effect: "drop",
            delay: 100,
            duration: 200,
            direction: "down"
        }
    });

    $( "button.slide" ).tooltip( "option", {
        show: {
            effect: "slide",
            delay: 250,
            duration: 350,
            direction: "left"
        },
        hide: {
            effect: "slide",
            delay: 150,
            duration: 350,
            direction: "right",
        }
    });

    $( "button.explode" ).tooltip( "option", {
        show: {
            effect: "clip",
```

```
            delay: 150,
            duration: 450
        },
        hide: {
            effect: "explode",
            delay: 200,
            duration: 1000
        }
    });

});
```

Look at the three buttons in your web browser and move the mouse over each one. You'll notice they each display and hide their tooltips in a unique fashion. For example, here is the last tooltip, mid-explosion as it's being hidden.

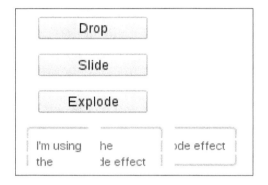

How it works...

Some effects accept options that others don't, such as direction. The `button.drop` tooltip widget is using the `drop` effect for both the show and hide actions. However, `show` is specifying the `direction` as up while the `hide` action specifies the `direction` as down. This means that the tooltip will enter the page in a upward motion, and will exit the page in a downward motion. The same concept applies to the `button.slide` widget where we're using the `slide` effect. The tooltip will slide in from the left, and will slide out to the right.

The `button.explode` tooltip is using two different effect types—show uses the `clip` effect while hide uses the `explode` effect. In general, mixing effects like this works fine, but often involves some trial and error time in finding two effect classes that complement one another as opposed to looking out of place. Lastly, we're applying the `delay` and `duration` options to the `show` and `hide` options for the tooltips we've created. The `delay` option postpones the actual display of the tooltip while the `duration` controls the runtime of the animation.

Tooltips for selected text

Most applications use terms that the user is encountering for the first time. And so, it's helpful to provide a glossary of sorts so they may look up the meaning of a new term. However, deciding on where to put this glossary inside the user interface is a big deal. For example, if I'm performing some task, I don't want to drop it to go look something up. This is where tooltips help—the user gets a contextual explanation of something.

Out of the box, tooltips work great when applied to a specific element on the page, such as a button or a progress bar. But what about paragraphs of text? Let's look at how we could allow the user to select some text, and display some contextual definition for the selection using the tooltip widget.

How to do it...

We'll design a new dictionary widget, based on the tooltip widget, used to work with text. This widget will handle text selection by displaying a tooltip with the appropriate tip if one is found. First, here are the paragraphs we'll use, taken from the preceding section.

```
<p>
    Most applications use terms that the user is encountering for the
first
    time.  And so, it's helpful to provide a glossary of sorts so they
may
    lookup the meaning of a new term.  However, deciding on where to
put this
    glossary inside the user interface is a big deal.  For example, if
I'm
    performing some task, I don't want to drop it to go look something
up.
    This is where tooltips help - the user gets a contextual
explanation
    of something.
</p>

<p>
    Out of the box, tooltips work great when applied to a specific
element on
    the page, such as a button or a progressbar. But what about
paragraphs of
    text?  Let's look at how we could allow the user to select some
text, and
    display some contextual definition for the selection using the
tooltip
    widget.
</p>
```

And here is the implementation of the dictionary widget, and how to apply it to our two paragraphs of text.

```
( function( $, undefined ) {

$.widget( "ab.dictionary", {

    options: {
        terms: []
    },

    ttPos: $.ui.tooltip.prototype.options.position,

    _create: function() {

        this._super();

        this._on({
            mouseup: this._tip,
            mouseenter: this._tip
        });

    },

    _destroy: function() {
        this._super();
        this._destroyTooltip();
    },

    _tip: function( e ) {

        var text = this._selectedText(),
            term = this._selectedTerm( text );

        if ( text === undefined || term === undefined ) {
            this._destroyTooltip();
            return;
        }

        if ( this.element.attr( "title" ) !== term.tip ) {
            this._destroyTooltip();
        }
```

```
        this._createTooltip( e, term );

    },

    _selectedText: function() {

        var selection, range, fragment;

        selection = window.getSelection();

        if ( selection.type !== "Range" ) {
            return;
        }

        range = selection.getRangeAt( 0 ),
        fragment = $( range.cloneContents() );

        return $.trim( fragment.text().toLowerCase() );

    },

    _selectedTerm: function( text ) {

        function isTerm( v ) {
            if ( v.term === text || v.term + "s" === text ) {
                return v;
            }
        }

        return $.map( this.options.terms, isTerm )[ 0 ];

    },

    _createTooltip: function( e, term ) {

        if ( this.element.is( ":ui-tooltip" ) ) {
            return;
        }

        var pos = $.extend( this.ttPos, { of: e } );

        this.element.attr( "title", term.tip )
                    .tooltip( { position: pos } )
                    .tooltip( "open" );
```

```
        },

    _destroyTooltip: function() {

        if ( !this.element.is( ":ui-tooltip" ) ) {
            return;
        }

        this.element.tooltip( "destroy" )
                    .attr( "title", "");

    }

});

})( jQuery );

$(function() {

    var dict = [
        {
            term: "tooltip",
            tip: "A contextual widget providing information to the
user"
        },
        {
            term: "progressbar",
            tip: "A widget illustrating the progress of some task"
        },
        {
            term: "element",
            tip: "An HTML element on the page"
        },
        {
            term: "user interface",
            tip: "Components on the screen the user interacts with"
        }
    ];

    $( "p" ).dictionary({
        terms: dict
    });

});
```

If you were to open this page in the browser and select "tooltips" using the mouse pointer, you should get a tooltip as is shown in the following screenshot:

Most applications use terms that the user is encountering for the first time. And so, it's helpful to provide a glossary of sorts so they may lookup the meaning of a new term. However, deciding on where to put this glossary inside the user interface is a big deal. For example, if I'm performing some task, I don't want to drop it to go look something up. This is where tooltips help – the user get's a contextual explanation of something.

Out of the box, tooltips work great when applied to a specific element on the page, such as a button or a progressbar. But what about paragraphs of text? Let's look at how we could allow the u   A contextual widget providing information to the   n for the selection using th   user

How it works...

Our new dictionary widget adds the ability for users to select paragraph text and get contextual definitions for their selection if one exists. The widget accepts a `terms` option, which is just an array of terms and tips. This is the dictionary data used to perform lookups when some text is selected. The `ttPos` attribute is a reference to the default tooltip `position` settings object. We keep this handy because we need to use it each time the user selects text and the tooltip widget is displayed. The `_create()` method, called when the widget is instantiated, sets up the event handling. In particular, we're interested in the `mouseup` and `mouseenter` events, both of which display the tooltip widget depending on a number of things. The `_destroy()` method makes sure that the tooltip widget we're using is also destroyed by calling `_destroyTooltip()`.

The `_tip()` method is like the main program, so to speak, of this widget as it ties together all the methods that have specific responsibilities. We get the selected text using the `_selectedText()` method. We get the selected term from the dictionary using the selected text. Now, either of these values may be undefined—the user may not have selected anything when `_tip()` is called, or the user has selected text that doesn't exist in the dictionary. If either case is true, we have to ensure that the tooltip is destroyed. If, on the other hand, a term is found, we create and display the tooltip using the `_createTooltip()` method.

The `_createTooltip()` method accepts an event object as well as a term object. The event object is used to position the tooltip when it is opened. Recall that we stored the default position options of the tooltip in the `ttPos` attribute. We create a new `position` object by extending the property with the event. This means that we can position the tooltip relative to where the user selected their text. Now that we've set the position on the tooltip, we just have to set the `title` attribute on the paragraph to the text we want displayed inside the tooltip. This is the `tip` attribute of the selected term passed into the method. The `_destroyTooltip()` takes care of both destroying the tooltip widget, but only if this element actually is a tooltip, and restoring the `title` attribute.

One final note, you'll notice that we're passing in simple terms strings to dictionary instances. But we're able to find several variants of the term in a given user selection. For example, "tooltips" will find the term "tooltip" because we're comparing with an added "s" in addition to the original string. We're also normalizing the white space on either side of the selection in addition to case insensitivity.

There's more...

The downside to our approach with the dictionary widget, where we make the user select the text in order to get a contextual definition for the word, is that the user doesn't know which words our dictionary defines. For example, the two paragraphs in the example define a grand total of four terms. For this to work, the user has to play a guessing game as to which text is actually defined. Further, selecting paragraph text is intuitive, but only if you frequently perform this action in the applications you use—most users do not.

Let's enhance our dictionary widget by introducing a new mode – hover. When this mode is true, we'll actually manipulate the paragraph text so that the terms defined within the dictionary stand out. The terms will look like links, and the tooltips containing the definition will behave like your typical tooltip. First, let's add this simple CSS rule that we'll apply to each term within the paragraph.

```
.ui-dictionary-term {
    text-decoration: underline;
    cursor: help;
}
```

We'll keep the same two paragraphs used previously, and the dictionary will be instantiated using the new mode option and we'll also modify the widget definition to make use of this new option. Here is the new JavaScript code:

```
( function( $, undefined ) {

$.widget( "ab.dictionary", {

    options: {
        terms: [],
        mode: "select"
    },

    ttPos: $.ui.tooltip.prototype.options.position,

    _create: function() {

        this._super();
```

```
    if ( this.options.mode === "select" ) {

        this._on({
            mouseup: this._tip,
            mouseenter: this._tip
        });

    }
    else if ( this.options.mode === "hover" ) {

        this._formatTerms();
        this._createTooltip();

    }

},

_destroy: function() {

    this._super();
    this._destroyTooltip();

    if ( this.options.mode === "hover" ) {
        this._unformatTerms();
    }

},

_tip: function( e ) {

    var text = this._selectedText(),
        term = this._selectedTerm( text );

    if ( text === undefined || term === undefined ) {
        this._destroyTooltip();
        return;
    }

    if ( this.element.attr( "title" ) !== term.tip ) {
        this._destroyTooltip();
    }

    this._createTooltip( e, term );
```

```
    },

    _selectedText: function() {

        var selection, range, fragement;

        selection = window.getSelection();

        if ( selection.type !== "Range" ) {
            return;
        }

        range = selection.getRangeAt( 0 ),
        fragment = $( range.cloneContents() );

        return $.trim( fragment.text().toLowerCase() );

    },

    _selectedTerm: function( text ) {

        function isTerm( v ) {
            if ( v.term === text || v.term + "s" === text ) {
                return v;
            }
        }

        return $.map( this.options.terms, isTerm )[ 0 ];

    },

    _createTooltip: function( e, term ) {

        if ( this.options.mode === "hover" ) {
            this.element.find( ".ui-dictionary-term" ).tooltip();
            return;
        }

        if ( this.element.is( ":ui-tooltip" ) ) {
            return;
        }

        var pos = $.extend( this.ttPos, { of: e } );
```

```
        this.element.attr( "title", term.tip )
                  .tooltip( { position: pos } )
                  .tooltip( "open" );

},

_destroyTooltip: function() {

    if( this.options.mode === "hover" ) {
        this.element.find( ".ui-dictionary-term" )
                  .tooltip( "destroy" );
        return;
    }

    if ( !this.element.is( ":ui-tooltip" ) ) {
        return;
    }

    this.element.tooltip( "destroy" )
              .attr( "title", "" );

},

_formatTerms: function() {

    function getTerm( v ) {
        return v.term;
    }

    var text = this.element.html(),
        terms = $.map( this.options.terms, getTerm );

    $.each( this.options.terms, function( i, v ) {

        var t = v.term,
            ex = new RegExp( "(" + t + "s|" + t + ")", "gi" ),
            termClass = "ui-dictionary-term",
            formatted = "<span " +
                        "class='" + termClass + "'" +
                        "title='" + v.tip + "'" +
                        ">$1</span>";

        text = text.replace( ex, formatted );

    });
```

```
            this.element.html( text );

        },

        _unformatTerms: function() {

            var $terms = this.element.find( ".ui-dictionary-term" );

            $terms.each( function( i, v ) {
                $( v ).replaceWith( $( v ).text() );
            });

        }

    });

})( jQuery );

$(function() {

    var dict = [
        {
            term: "tooltip",
            tip: "A contextual widget providing information to the
user"
        },
        {
            term: "progressbar",
            tip: "A widget illustrating the progress of some task"
        },
        {
            term: "element",
            tip: "An HTML element on the page"
        },
        {
            term: "user interface",
            tip: "Components on the screen the user interacts with"
        }
    ]

    $( "p" ).dictionary({
        terms: dict,
        mode: "hover"
    });

});
```

Now, when you look at the two paragraphs in the browser, you'll notice that the terms we have defined in the dictionary data are underlined. So when the user hovers their mouse pointer over the term, they get the help cursor icon, along with the tooltip.

Most applications use terms that the user is encountering for the first time. And so, it's helpful to provide a glossary of sorts so they may lookup the meaning of a new term. However, deciding on where to put this glossary inside the user interface is a big deal. For example, if I'?performing some task, I don't want to drop it to go look something up. This is where tooltips help – the user get's a contextual explanation of something.

Out of the box, as a button or could allow th selection using the tooltip widget.

A contextual widget providing information to the user

ie page, such at how we ition for the

The new `mode` option we've introduced to the dictionary widget accepts a string value of either `select` or `hover`—it defaults to `select`, which is the behavior we had originally implemented in this example. In the widget constructor, the `_create()` method, we're checking the `mode` value. If we're in the `hover` mode, we call the `_formatTerms()` method which changes the visual appearance of the terms inside the paragraph. Next, we call `_createTooltip()`, the same method used in the original implementation except that it too is now mode-aware. The `_formatTerms()` stores the text of the given element and then iterates through the dictionary terms. For each term, it builds a regular expression and replaces any found terms with a `span` element used to create the tooltips.

12
Widgets and More!

In this chapter, we will cover the following recipes:

- ► Accordions to tabs, and back again
- ► Building a custom widget from scratch
- ► Building an observer widget
- ► Using widgets with Backbone applications

Introduction

Until now, each chapter in this book has focused on working with a specific widget that ships with jQuery UI. In this chapter, we're more interested in the grand scheme of things. After all, you're building an application, and not a demonstration. So, it's important that developers using jQuery UI be conscious not only about how each individual widget works on their own, but also about how they behave in their environment, and how they interact with other widgets and frameworks.

We'll also address the nuts-and-bolts of the framework in this chapter by building a widget from the ground up, with the help of the widget factory. With the generic widget machinery at your disposal, you could write a handful of widgets that have nothing to do with the default widgets. Although these custom widgets don't inherit much functionality, they behave like jQuery UI widgets, and that alone is worth the effort—cementing a layer of consistency into your application.

Accordions to tabs, and back again

Both the accordion and the tabs widgets are containers. That is, their typical use inside the context of an application is to organize subcomponents. These subcomponents might be other widgets, or any other HTML element for that matter. So, both widgets fit the generic description of a container, that is, a widget with different sections. There are obviously subtleties to that description; for example, accordions don't support remote Ajax content. Also, the way users traverse the sections are quite different. Yet, they're essentially interchangeable. Why not introduce the ability to switch between the two widgets, especially during run time where the users can set their own preference and toggle between the two containers? It turns out that we can implement something like this. Let's look at how we would go about doing this. We need a bidirectional conversion between the two widgets. That way, the tabs widget can be transformed into an accordion widget, and vice-versa.

How to do it...

To implement the kind of transformation between two different widgets we're talking about here, we'll have to extend both the accordion and the tabs widget. We'll add a new method to each of the widgets that converts the widget to its counterpart. Here is the HTML structure we'll need to make this example happen:

```html
<button class="toggle">Toggle</button>

<div id="accordion">
    <h3>Section 1</h3>
    <div>
        <p>Section 1 content...</p>
    </div>
    <h3>Section 2</h3>
    <div>
        <p>Section 2 content...</p>
    </div>
    <h3>Section 3</h3>
    <div>
        <p>Section 3 content...</p>
    </div>
</div>

<button class="toggle">Toggle</button>

<div id="tabs">
    <ul>
        <li><a href="#section1">Section 1</a></li>
```

```
        <li><a href="#section2">Section 2</a></li>
        <li><a href="#section3">Section 3</a></li>
    </ul>
    <div id="section1">
        <p>Section 1 content...</p>
    </div>
    <div id="section2">
        <p>Section 2 content...</p>
    </div>
    <div id="section3">
        <p>Section 3 content...</p>
    </div>
</div>
```

Here, we have two toggle buttons, an accordion `div` and a tabs `div`. The toggle buttons will morph their corresponding container widget, into another widget type. Here is the JavaScript code:

```
( function( $, undefined ) {

$.widget( "ab.accordion", $.ui.accordion, {

    tabs: function() {

        this.destroy();

        var self = this,
            oldHeaders = this.headers,
            newHeaders = $( "<ul/>" );

        oldHeaders.each( function( i, v ) {

            var id = self.namespace + "-tabs-" + self.uuid + "-" + i,
                header = $( "<li/>" ).appendTo( newHeaders );

            $( "<a/>" ).text( $( v ).text() )
                    .attr( "href", "#" + id )
                    .appendTo( header );

            oldHeaders.next().eq( i ).attr( "id", id );

        });

        newHeaders.prependTo(this.element);
```

```
            this.headers.remove();
            return this.element.tabs();

        }

    });

    $.widget( "ab.tabs", $.ui.tabs, {

        accordion: function() {

            this.destroy();

            var self = this;

            this.tabs.each( function( i, v ) {

                var $link = $( v ).find( "a" ),
                    id = $link.attr( "href" ),
                    text = $link.text();

                $( "<h3/>" ).text( text )
                        .insertBefore( id );

            });

            this.tablist.remove();
            return this.element.accordion();

        },

    });

})( jQuery );

$(function() {

    $( "button.toggle" ).button().on( "click", function( e ) {

        var $widget = $( this ).next();

        if ( $widget.is( ":ab-accordion" ) ) {
            $widget.accordion( "tabs" );
```

```
        }
        else if ( $widget.is( ":ab-tabs" ) ) {
            $widget.tabs( "accordion" );
        }

    });

    $( "#accordion" ).accordion();
    $( "#tabs" ).tabs();

});
```

How it works...

When the page first loads and all the DOM elements are ready, we create the toggle button widgets, an accordion widget, and a tabs widget. This is illustrated in the following screenshot:

Now, clicking on the top toggle button will transform the accordion widget into a tabs widget. Also, the second toggle button will transform the tabs widget into an accordion. Here is the result of clicking on each of the toggle buttons once:

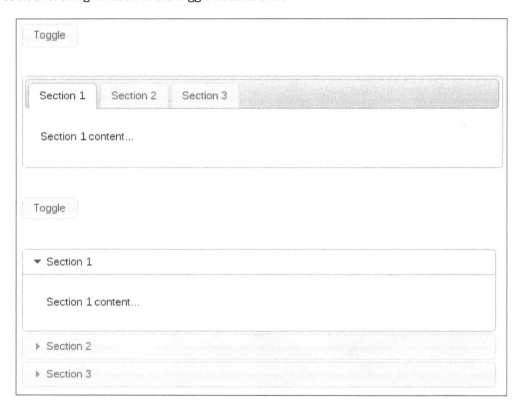

The toggle buttons work by using jQuery's `next()` function to grab the next widget, either `#accordion` or `#tabs`, depending on the button clicked. This is then stored in the `$widget` variable because we access it several times. Firstly, we check if the widget is an accordion, and if so, we call the `tabs()` method on the accordion. Likewise, if `$widget` is tabs, we call the `accordion()` method to transform it. Notice that we're using the built-in widget selector that the widget factory creates for each widget in order to determine what kind of widget the element is. Also, notice that the namespace is `ab`, not `ui`, which is the recommended practice when writing your own widgets, or customizing existing widgets, as is the case here. Here, I've chosen my initials as the namespace. In practice, this would be a standard convention that somehow relates to the application.

Let's now turn our attention to the `tabs()` method we've added to the accordion widget. The essential job of this new method is to destroy the accordion widget, manipulate the DOM elements so as to take on a form that the tabs widget will recognize, and then to instantiate the tabs widget. So, this is what we do, we call the `destroy()` method first. Notice, however, that we still have access to some of the attributes of the accordion widget, such as `headers`. Destroying a widget is mainly concerned with removing any adornments introduced into the DOM as a result of creating the widget in the first place, in addition to removing the event handlers. It doesn't, at the JavaScript level, care much about destroying the widget object that we're working with here.

At this point, we have the `oldHeaders` variable, which points to the original accordion's h3 elements. Next, we have `newHeaders`, which is an empty `ul` element. The `newHeaders` element is the starting point for the new elements the tab widget expects to find. Next, we have to build the `li` elements that point to the content panels of the tabs. For each header, we add a link to the `newHeaders ul`. But, we also have to update the panel ID with an `id` that the header links to. We first build an ID string using the position of the tab as well as the `uuid` of the widget itself. The uuid isn't strictly necessary; however, it's a good idea nonetheless to ensure unique tab IDs.

Lastly, we add the new headers to the element, and remove the old headers. At this point, we have enough to instantiate a tabs widget. And that's just what we do. Notice that we return the newly-created object, so that if it is referenced elsewhere in the code, it can be replaced by this method, for example, `myTabs = myAccordion.accordion( "tabs" )`.

The `accordion()` method we've added to the tabs widget follows the same principles applied in the `tabs()` method described above—we want to destroy the widget, manipulate the DOM, and create the accordion widget. To make this happen, we need to insert the h3 header element before the corresponding content panel. We then remove the `tablist` element, and the tabs `ul`, followed by a call to instantiate and return the accordion widget.

Building a custom widget from scratch

The most powerful aspect of jQuery UI isn't the prebuilt widgets that ship with it, but rather, the machinery used to build those widgets. Each widget shares a common infrastructure called the widget factory, and this is exposed to developers using the framework. The widget factory provides a means for developers to define their own widgets. We've already glimpsed the widget factory in action throughout this book. We've been using it to extend the capabilities of any given widget. The focus of this section takes on a different perspective of the widget factory. That is, how can we use it to build our own widgets from the ground up?

Well, we don't want to start with nothing, as that would defeat the whole purpose of the widget factory. Instead, the aim when building any widget is to utilize the generic capabilities that the base widget class makes available. In addition, there are some basic design principles that developers should try to stick with when they're creating widgets. For example, your widget should perform clean up when destroyed, removing attributes, event handlers, and essentially leaving the element as you found it. Widgets should also provide a simple API, and it should be clear to the developers using your widget what it does, and more importantly, what it does not do. Let's touch on some principles to keep in mind before you start, and while designing your widget:

- ▶ **Keep it simple**: with the latest version of jQuery UI, a number of the standard widgets have undergone major refactoring work in an effort to simplify their interfaces. Borrow from this lesson when designing your widgets and keep their responsibilities to a minimum. It can be tempting, during the implementation phase of the widget, to decide that you need to add another method to the API, perhaps several. Think long and hard before doing this, because making the API larger generally leads to a widget that is difficult to maintain and keep stable. And that is the whole idea behind widgets, a small modular component that is reliable, and can be used in a variety of contexts without blowing up. With that said, a widget that doesn't meet the needs of the application isn't of any value either.

- ▶ **Design for extensibility**: Building on the keep it simple principle is that of extensibility. Again, as we've seen throughout this book, extensibility is often key in giving the widget extra capabilities the application needs to do its job. These can be simple customizations, or a complete re-write of a method. Regardless, assume that your widget will be modified, and that it will have observers listening for events. In other words, a good widget will provide a reasonable level of granularity with regards to how functionality is distributed among the methods that realize it. Each method is an entry point for specialization, and so the potential entry points should be a conscious concern. Events triggered by the widget communicate the state of the widget to the outside world. So when the state of your widget changes, be sure to let everyone else know about it.

How to do it...

Enough talk already—now, let's build a checklist widget. It really is as simple as it sounds. We'll base the widget on a `ul` element, which will transform each `li` element into a checklist item. The checklist won't just sit there by itself though; we'll add a few external components to interact with our widget. We'll want a button that adds a new checklist item, a button that removes an item, and a progressbar for tracking the progress of our list. The main user interaction with the widget itself is centered on checking and unchecking items.

Here is the HTML we'll use in this example:

```
<div class="container">
    <button id="add">Add</button>
```

```
        <button id="remove">Remove</button>
    </div>
    <div class="container">
        <ul id="checklist">
            <li><a href="#">Write some code</a></li>
            <li><a href="#">Deploy some code</a></li>
            <li><a href="#">Fix some code</a></li>
            <li><a href="#">Write some new code</a></li>
        </ul>
    </div>
    <div class="container">
        <div id="progressbar"></div>
    </div>
```

Next, we'll add the CSS required by our checklist widget.

```
.ui-checklist {
    list-style-type: none;
    padding: 0.2em;
}

.ui-checklist li {
    padding: 0.4em;
    border: 1px solid transparent;
    cursor: pointer;
}

.ui-checklist li a {
    text-decoration: none;
    outline: none;
}

.ui-checklist-checked {
    text-decoration: line-through;
}
```

Finally, we'll add our widget definition using the following JavaScript code. This code also creates the two button widgets and the progressbar widget used in this example.

```
( function( $, undefined ) {

$.widget( "ab.checklist", {

    options: {
        items: "> li",
        widgetClasses: [
```

```
            "ui-checklist",
            "ui-widget",
            "ui-widget-content",
            "ui-corner-all"
        ],
        itemClasses: [
            "ui-checklist-item",
            "ui-corner-all"
        ],
        checkedClass: "ui-checklist-checked"
    },

    _getCreateEventData: function() {

        var items = this.items,
            checkedClass = this.options.checkedClass;

        return {
            items: items.length,
            checked: items.filter( "." + checkedClass ).length
        }

    },

    _create: function() {

        this._super();

        var classes = this.options.widgetClasses.join( " " );

        this.element.addClass( classes );

        this._on({
            "click .ui-checklist-item": this._click,
        });

        this.refresh();

    },

    _destroy: function() {

        this._super();
```

```
        var widgetClasses = this.options.widgetClasses.join( " " ),
            itemClasses = this.options.itemClasses.join( " " ),
            checkedClass = this.options.checkedClass;

        this.element.removeClass( widgetClasses );

        this.items.removeClass( itemClasses )
                .removeClass( checkedClass )
                .removeAttr( "aria-checked" );

    },

    _click: function( e ) {

        e.preventDefault();
        this.check( this.items.index( $( e.currentTarget ) ) );

    },

    refresh: function() {

        var trigger = true,
            items,
            newItems;

        if ( this.items === undefined ) {
            trigger = false;
            this.items = $();
        }

        items = this.element.find( this.options.items )
        newItems = items.not( this.items );

        items.addClass( this.options.itemClasses.join( " " ) );

        this._hoverable( newItems );
        this._focusable( newItems );

        this.items = items;

        if ( trigger ) {
            this._trigger( "refreshed",
                        null,
                        this._getCreateEventData() );
```

```
            }

        },

    check: function( index ) {

        var $item = this.items.eq( index ),
            checked;

        if ( !$item.length ) {
            return;
        }

        checked = $item.attr( "aria-checked" ) === "true" ?
                "false" : "true";

        $item.toggleClass( this.options.checkedClass )
            .attr( "aria-checked", checked );

        this._trigger( "checked", null, this._getCreateEventData());

    }

});

})( jQuery );

$(function() {

    $( "#add" ).button({
        icons: {
            primary: "ui-icon-plus"
        },
        text: false
    });

    $( "#add" ).on( "click", function( e ) {

        var $checklist = $( "#checklist" ),
            $item = $( "<li/>" ).appendTo( checklist );

        $( "<a/>" ).attr( "href", "#" )
                .text( "Write some documentation" )
                .appendTo( $item );
```

```
            $checklist.checklist( "refresh" );

    });

    $( "#remove" ).button({
        icons: {
            primary: "ui-icon-minus"
        },
        text: false
    });

    $( "#remove" ).on( "click", function( e ) {

        var $checklist = $( "#checklist" ),
            $item = $checklist.find( ".ui-checklist-item:last" );

        $item.remove();
        $checklist.checklist( "refresh" );

    });

    $( "#progressbar" ).progressbar();

    $( "#checklist" ).checklist({
        create: function( e, ui ) {
            $( "#progressbar" ).progressbar( "option", {
                max: ui.items,
                value: ui.checked
            });
        },
        refreshed: function( e, ui ) {
            $( "#progressbar" ).progressbar( "option", {
                max: ui.items,
                value: ui.checked
            });
        },
        checked: function( e, ui ) {
            $( "#progressbar" ).progressbar( "value", ui.checked );
        }
    });

});
```

When you first load the page, the checklist widget, along with the other components on the page, should look something like this:

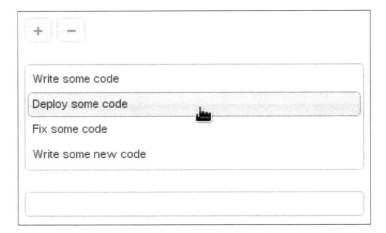

You can see that these are the default checklist items as specified in the HTML structure. The hover state works as expected, but the progressbar is at 0. This is because the checklist doesn't have any selected items. Let's check some items off, and add some more.

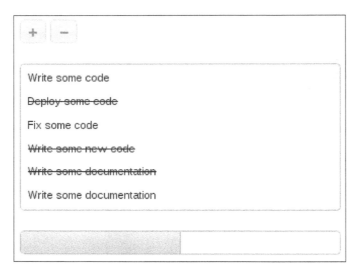

You can see that the progress bar is updated each time an item is added or removed from the checklist, as well as when an individual item is checked or unchecked.

How it works...

Let's first discuss the HTML structure of the checklist widget along with the new CSS required to display it. We'll then divide the definition and instantiation of the widget into sections and conquer those. The HTML used in this example is divided into three main container `div` elements. The first element holds our add and remove item buttons. The second one is for the checklist widget, and the last one is for the progressbar. That is the general layout.

The most important aspect of the HTML structure is the `#container` element, which is the foundation of our checklist widget. Each item is stored inside an `li` element. Notice that the text of the item is wrapped in an `a` element as well. This makes dealing with focusing the individual items, when the user is tabbing through the page elements, much simpler to deal with. The main styles of the checklist are controlled by the `ui-checklist` class. This class gets applied to the element when the widget is first created, and it performs some standard style manipulations for lists, like removing the bulleted images. Another thing we need to handle is the border spacing, which becomes relevant when the user hovers over an item, and `ui-state-hover` is added and removed. The `a` elements, wrapping the item text, don't need any text decoration since we're not using them as standard links. Finally, the `ui-checklist-checked` class is relevant to the state of an individual checklist item and visually marks the item as checked. It also serves as a query helper when we need to collect all checked items.

Let's now turn our attention to the widget definition, and how we're instantiating and using it.

- ▶ **The options**: The first thing our widget defines are its options, each with a default value. Always make sure that any option you add to a widget has a default value, as we can never rely on one being supplied during the time of creation. The options we define here for our checklist widget are fairly simple, and will rarely be changed by the developer. For example, the items we look up will generally always be `li` elements. And, the classes we've defined here, that get applied to the widget itself, probably will never change. However, they need to be declared somewhere, and so we can hard code it, or put them somewhere the developer has access to. Think of options as attributes, or properties of the widget object.

- ▶ **The private methods**: By convention, the private methods, or methods that don't make up part of the API visible to the user, are prefixed with an underscore. Our first private method is the `_getCreateEventData()` method. This is called internally by the base widget class when the create event for the widget is triggered. This method is a hook for allowing us to supply custom data to the create event handlers. All we're doing here is passing an object that has the number of items stored in the items attribute, and the number of checked items stored in the checked attribute.

▶ **The create method**: The `_create()` method is probably the most common method for any widget, since it's called by the widget factory as the widgets constructor. We're using the `_super()` utility method to call the base widget constructor for us, which performs some boilerplate initialization work for us. Next, we apply the relevant widget CSS classes to the element using the `widgetClasses` option. Next, we use the `_on()` method to setup an event handler for the click event. Notice that we're passing in a delegate selector after the event name. `ui-checklist-item`. The reason we're doing this is because items can be added, and items can be removed from the checklist, and so it makes sense to use this approach rather than manually managing the click events for each item.

▶ **The destroy method**: The `_destroy()` method is essential, as previously mentioned, to performing clean up tasks. We use `_super()` here to call the base widget `_destroy()` method which will clean up any event handlers we've created using `_on()`. Then, we just need to remove any classes and attributes that we've added throughout the lifespan of the widget. The last of the private methods is the `_click()` method, the even handler bound to the click event when the widget was first created. The job of this method is to change the state of the clicked item, and we do this by calling the `check()` method, part of the API exposed to developers. We also want to prevent the default action of the link clicks here, because they have the potential to reload the page.

▶ **The API**: In the spirit of keeping our widget simple, the exposed API consists of only two methods. The first one is the `refresh()` method, which is responsible for locating the items that make up our checklist. These are stored in the `items` attribute of the widget object, which is an example of something that isn't exposed through the API. The `items` attribute is only used internally; however, if a developer were to extend our widget, their custom methods would be accessible, and perhaps even useful. The `refresh()` method changes the state of the widget when new items are found, and this is why it triggers the refreshed event. However, there is a corner case during which we don't want to trigger this event, and that is when the widget is being instantiated for the first time. This is tracked in the `trigger` variable (if we haven't stored any items yet, then it's safe to assume that we're creating, and not refreshing it). The reason we don't want to collide with the create event is that this is very misleading for developers using the widget. We're also using the `_hoverable()`, and `_focusable()` methods on each newly-found item. This is a standard widget pattern for items within a widget that the user interacts with.

▶ **The check method**: The `check()` method is the other half of the checklist API, and it too changes the state of the widget. It fires a changed event, which includes data about the item count and the checked count, same as the created event data. You'll notice that this method ensures the handling of the appropriate `aria` attributes, as do the standard jQuery UI widgets. The `aria` standard promotes accessibility, which is why the jQuery UI framework uses it, and our widget shouldn't be any different. Finally, it is the job of this method to toggle the class of this item, using the value stored in the `checkedClass` option.

> ▶ **The main application**: When the page loads, the first thing we do is create our two button widgets: #add and #remove. The #add button, when clicked, adds a new item DOM element to the checklist. It then uses the refresh() method to update the state of the widget, as well as trigger any events. Likewise, the #remove button removes a DOM element, and calls the refresh() method, triggering any state change behavior. The progressbar widget is instantiated without any options, as it knows nothing about our checklist widget.

Lastly, our checklist widget is created with three options. These are all event handlers, and they all share the same responsibility—update the #progressbar widget. For example, the widget is first created, and the progressbar is updated with the items found in the DOM (nothing has been checked yet). The refreshed event is triggered when new items are added or removed from the list; we want to update the progressbar here too. The checked event handler fires anytime the user checks or unchecks an item, and here, we're only interested in updating the value for the progressbar since the total number of items is the same.

Building an observer widget

The typical approach to dealing with events triggered by jQuery UI widgets is to bind an event handler to that event name, passed directly into the constructor. It's the typical approach because it's easy to do, and it generally solves a specific problem we're having. For example, suppose that when a section of our accordion widget is expanded, we would like to update another DOM element. To do this, assign an event handler function to the activate event when the accordion is constructed.

This approach works well for small, single purpose jobs that apply to a single instance of a given widget. However, most meaningful applications have many widgets, all triggering their own events. The widget factory prefixes each event with the name of the widget, which generally means that even outside of the widget context we know what we're working with. This is especially helpful when we want to bind event handlers to widget events, long after the widget has been created.

Let's build an **observer** widget that will help us visualize all the potential widget events taking place in an application. The observer widget is capable of binding to a single widget, to a group of widgets, or the entire document. We'll look at the latter case, where the observer will even pick up events for widgets created in the future.

How to do it...

Let's take a look at the CSS styles used by the observer widget first:

```
.ui-observer-event {
    padding: 1px;
}
```

```css
.ui-observer-event-border {
    border-bottom: 1px solid;
}

.ui-observer-event-timestamp {
    float: right;
}
```

Now, let's look at the HTML used to create a basic page with a few sample widgets on it. These widgets will trigger the events we're trying to pick up with our observer.

```html
<div class="container">
    <h1 class="ui-widget">Accordion</h1>
    <div id="accordion">
        <h3>Section 1</h3>
        <div>
            <p>Section 1 content</p>
        </div>
        <h3>Section 2</h3>
        <div>
            <p>Section 2 content</p>
        </div>
    </div>
</div>
<div class="container">
    <h1 class="ui-widget">Menu</h1>
    <ul id="menu">
        <li><a href="#">Item 1</a></li>
        <li><a href="#">Item 2</a></li>
        <li><a href="#">Item 3</a></li>
    </ul>
</div>
<div class="container">
    <h1 class="ui-widget">Tabs</h1>
    <div id="tabs">
        <ul>
            <li><a href="#tab1">Tab 1</a></li>
            <li><a href="#tab2">Tab 2</a></li>
            <li><a href="#tab3">Tab 3</a></li>
        </ul>
        <div id="tab1">
            <p>Tab 1 content</p>
        </div>
        <div id="tab2">
```

```
        <p>Tab 2 content</p>
      </div>
      <div id="tab3">
          <p>Tab 3 content</p>
      </div>
    </div>
  </div>
```

Finally, here is what the implementation of the widget looks like, along with the four widget instances used on this page:

```
( function( $, undefined ) {

$.widget( "ab.observer", {

    options: {

        observables: [
            {
                widget: $.ui.accordion,
                events: [
                    "activate",
                    "beforeActivate",
                    "create"
                ]
            },
            {
                widget: $.ui.menu,
                events: [
                    "blur",
                    "create",
                    "focus",
                    "select"
                ]
            },
            {
                widget: $.ui.tabs,
                events: [
                    "activate",
                    "beforeActivate",
                    "create"
                ]
            }
        ]
```

```
    },

    _getEvents: function() {

        var events = {};

        $.each( this.options.observables, function ( i, v ) {

            var prefix = v.widget.prototype.widgetEventPrefix;

            $.each( v.events, function( i, v ) {
                events[ prefix + v.toLowerCase() ] = "_event";
            });

        });

        return events;

    },

    _create: function() {

        this._super();

        var dialogId = "ui-observer-dialog-" + this.uuid,
            dialogSettings = {
                minHeight: 300,
                maxHeight: 300,
                position: {
                    my: "right top",
                    at: "right top"
                },
                title: this.element.selector
            };

        this.dialog = $( "<div/>" ).attr( "id", dialogId )
                                   .attr( "title", "Observer" )
                                   .addClass( "ui-observer" )
                                   .appendTo( "body" )
                                   .dialog( dialogSettings );

        this._on( this.element, this._getEvents() );

    },
```

```
_event: function( e, ui ) {

    var eventClasses = "ui-observer-event " +
                        "ui-observer-event-border",
        $event = $( "<div/>" ).prependTo( this.dialog )
                            .addClass( eventClasses ),
        time = new Date( e.timeStamp ).toLocaleTimeString();

    $( "<span/>" ).html( e.type )
                .appendTo( $event );

    $( "<span/>" ).html( time )
                .addClass( "ui-observer-event-timestamp" )
                .appendTo( $event );

    this.dialog.find( ".ui-observer-event:last" )
                .removeClass( "ui-observer-event-border" );

},

_destroy: function() {

    this._super();
    this.dialog.dialog( "destroy" )
                .remove();

}

});

})( jQuery );

$(function() {

    $( document ).observer();

    $( "#accordion" ).accordion();
    $( "#menu" ).menu();
    $( "#tabs" ).tabs();

});
```

Looking at this page in the browser, the basic widget layout looks something along the lines of the following screenshot:

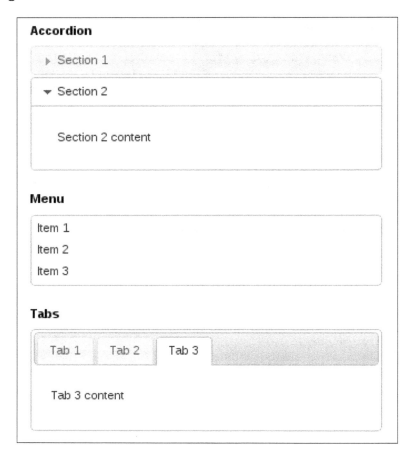

Even simply creating these widgets will trigger events. For example, when the page first loads, you'll see that the dialog created by the observer widget is already populated with events.

How it works...

The observable widget, in this example, is applied to the `document` element. This means that it will pick up any widget events that bubble up to that level. The observable widget defines an `observables` option, an array of widgets whose events we'd like to listen to. In this case, for the sake of brevity, we're only including three widgets. This can always be extended, as needed by the application, since it is an option.

The purpose of the `_getEvents()` method is to read the `observables` option and to build an object that we can use to bind these events to the `_event()` method. Notice that we're automatically adding the widget prefix value to the event name here—this is available in the `widgetEventPrefix` property of the widget prototype. The job of the `_create()` method is to insert a `div` element into the `body` element, which then becomes a dialog widget. We position it in the top-right of the page so as to get out of the user's way. Finally, we start listening for events using the object returned by `_getEvents()` using the `_on()` method.

The `_event()` method is the single callback used anytime one of the widget events we're listening to is fired. It simply logs the event to the observer dialog. It also logs the time of the event; so, this tool is useful for experimenting with any jQuery UI application, large or small, since it can highlight which events actually take place, along with their orderings. The widget also takes care to destroy the dialog widget it created earlier too.

Using widgets with Backbone applications

With the seemingly endless variations of JavaScript environments you may find yourself working in, it's best to embrace the fact that not everything is done the jQuery UI way. If you find yourself on a project where you're just itching to use jQuery UI widgets, because the use cases are plentiful, you'll have to take the time necessary in understanding the consequences of jQuery UI mingling with another framework.

It's generally ill-advised for any developer to mix completely different widget frameworks together, so hopefully that is something easily avoided. You'll of course have to work other homebrew HTML and CSS concoctions, but this is typical. It is not so bad, as you can control it (not easily done with other open source frameworks). So, if not other widget frameworks, what other frameworks might we have to consider working with?

Backbone is a general framework that builds on the lower-level `underscore.js` utility library, for adding structure to web application clients. You'll find concepts such as models, collections, and views in a Backbone application. A full treatment of the Backbone library is way beyond the scope of this book. But, it's helpful to think of Backbone as the application scaffolding, the part that doesn't change. It'll run just the same with or without jQuery UI widgets. But, since jQuery UI is what we're interested in working with, let's build ourselves a little Backbone application that uses jQuery UI widgets.

How to do it...

The goal of the application is to display an autocomplete widget, where the user can filter programming language names. When a selection is made, some details about the language are displayed, including a delete button, which deletes the language from the collection. Simple, right? Let's get into it.

In the page header, we'll be doing something different—including a template. Templates are just strings of text, rendered by Backbone views. We'll give it a type of `text/template`, so the browser will not try to interpret it as something other than a template (JavaScript code, for instance). It has an `id`, so we can reference the template text later when it's time to render the template.

```
<script type="text/template" id="template-detail">
    <div>
        <strong>Title: </strong>
        <span><%= title %></span>
    </div>
    <div>
        <strong>Authors: </strong>
        <span><%= authors %></span>
    </div>
    <div>
```

```
            <strong>Year: </strong>
            <span><%= year %></span>
        </div>
        <div>
            <button class="delete">Delete</button>
        </div>
    </script>
```

Next, the minimal CSS used by this UI—simple font and layout adjustments.

```
.search, .detail {
    margin: 20px;
}

.detail {
    font-size: 1.4em;
}

.detail button {
    font-size: 0.8em;
    margin-top: 5px;
}
```

Next, we have the actual markup used by the user interface. Notice how minimal the `detail` class `div` is. That's because it's simply a holder for the template, rendered by the view, as we'll see in a moment.

```
<div class="search">
    <label for="search">Search:</label>
    <input id="search"/>
</div>
<div class="detail"></div>
```

Finally, we have the actual Backbone application that uses the autocomplete and button jQuery UI widgets.

 For brevity, we're cutting out the bulk of the code listing here, trying to just show the essentials. The fully-operational Backbone code is available for download, along with all the other samples in this book.

```
$(function() {

    // Model and collection classes

    var Language,
        LanguageCollection;
```

```
// View classes

var AutocompleteView,
    LanguageView;

// Application router

var AppRouter;

// Collection instance

var languages;

// Application and view instances

var app,
    searchView,
    detailView;

/**
 *
 * Class definitions
 *
 **/

Language = Backbone.Model.extend({
    // ...
});

LanguageCollection = Backbone.Collection.extend({
    // ...
});

AutocompleteView = Backbone.View.extend({
    // ...
});

LanguageView = Backbone.View.extend({
    // ...
});

AppRouter = Backbone.Router.extend({

});

/**
 *
 * Collection, view, and application instances
```

```
    *
    **/

    languages = new LanguageCollection([
        // …
    ]);

    searchView = new AutocompleteView({
        // ….
    });

    detailView = new LanguageView({
        // …
    });

    app = new AppRouter();

    Backbone.history.start();

});
```

Running this example will present the user with an autocomplete `input` element. The details of the chosen language are shown in the following screenshot:

How it works...

Our entire Backbone application is declared within the document ready callback function. Once that is done, everything is event-based. Let's step through the application components. The first thing you'll notice is that we've declared our variables up top, and given them brief categorical explanations. This is often helpful when we're sharing the same namespace with more than a handful of variables. The categories are as follows:

▶ **Model and collection classes**: The classes used by our application to define the data model.

▶ **View classes**: Classes used by our application to provide the user with different views of the data model.

- ▶ **Application router**: A single controller-like class that manipulates the browser address, and executes relevant functionality when the path changes.

- ▶ **Collection instance**: A collection instance represents the application data – a collection of model instances.

- ▶ **Application and view instances**: The single application, along with the various views used by that application to present data.

With that in mind, let's now dive into the specifics of how each Backbone class works. The application has only one model class, `Language`. We can see here that the `Language` declaration defines some default values for the attributes once instantiated. Next, the `LanguageCollection` class is an extension of the Backbone Collection class. This is where all our `Language` instances go. Notice that we're specifying the model property to point to the `Language` class. Since we have no RESTful API, we have to tell the collection that any synchronization actions should be carried out locally. We have to include the local storage plugin for Backbone in order to make this happen. This is actually an ideal way to bootstrap UI development before the real backend is completely fleshed out.

Next, we have our first view class, `AutocompleteView`, which is specific to the autocomplete jQuery UI widget. We've named it as such because we've done our best here to make it generic enough that it could be used with another autocomplete widget. We do have some language specifics hard-coded in the view class, but these are trivial to improve upon should the need arise. The first property defined in this class is the `events` object. These are mostly related to the autocomplete widget events. Each callback event handler is defined as a view method below. The `initialize()` method is the view constructor, and it is here that we call `delegateEvents()` to activate our events handlers for current elements, as well as future elements. The constructor then creates the autocomplete widget, and listens to its connection for destroy events.

The `autocompleteCreate()` method is fired after the autocomplete widget is created, and assigns the `source` option of the widget. This is a proxy to the `autocompleteSource` method of this view. The `autocompleteSelect` method fires when the user selects an item, and navigates to the appropriate route. The `autocompleteChange()` method is fired when the autocomplete widget loses focus and the item is different. We do this to update the path if the user has removed his/her previous selection. The `keyup()` handler exists to handle the route change when the user has removed their selection, but hasn't yet blurred the autocomplete focus. Lastly, the `autocompleteSearch()` method is how the autocomplete widget is populated with items when the user starts typing. First, we perform a filter, using the underscore `filter()` method on the collection, then we map using the underscore `map()` method on the collection. The mapping is necessary to return a format the autocomplete widget expects.

The next crucial piece of our application is the `LanguageView` class, responsible for rendering the programming language details. Like the previous view, this one sets up event handlers using the `events` property. We're also using the `#template-detail` text mentioned earlier, to compile the template rendered by this view using the underscore template machinery. In the constructor, we're listing some events on the collection of this view. One event to take note of is the `change:selected` event. This will only fire when the `selected` attribute changes, which is good, because that's all we're interested in.

The `render()` method is responsible for rendering the template, but only if the model in question is actually selected. Once rendered, we can instantiate the button widget used by this view. However, take note that the event handler isn't bound again for the click event since that was delegated when the view was first created.

The `AppRouter` class is the application controller in that it is responsible for reacting to changes in the URL path. The `routeLang()` method responds to a specific language and marks it as selected. The `routeDefault()` method handles all other requests. Its only job is to make sure that no languages are marked as selected, and as a side effect, any previously-selected languages will be removed from the UI since `LanguageView` is listening for changes in the `selected` attribute.

Finally, we create instances of our model in the collection instance, and then, our views and the application router.

Index

Symbols

X

Thank you for buying
jQuery UI Cookbook

About Packt Publishing

Packt, pronounced 'packed', published its first book "*Mastering phpMyAdmin for Effective MySQL Management*" in April 2004 and subsequently continued to specialize in publishing highly focused books on specific technologies and solutions.

Our books and publications share the experiences of your fellow IT professionals in adapting and customizing today's systems, applications, and frameworks. Our solution based books give you the knowledge and power to customize the software and technologies you're using to get the job done. Packt books are more specific and less general than the IT books you have seen in the past. Our unique business model allows us to bring you more focused information, giving you more of what you need to know, and less of what you don't.

Packt is a modern, yet unique publishing company, which focuses on producing quality, cutting-edge books for communities of developers, administrators, and newbies alike. For more information, please visit our website: www.packtpub.com.

About Packt Open Source

In 2010, Packt launched two new brands, Packt Open Source and Packt Enterprise, in order to continue its focus on specialization. This book is part of the Packt Open Source brand, home to books published on software built around Open Source licences, and offering information to anybody from advanced developers to budding web designers. The Open Source brand also runs Packt's Open Source Royalty Scheme, by which Packt gives a royalty to each Open Source project about whose software a book is sold.

Writing for Packt

We welcome all inquiries from people who are interested in authoring. Book proposals should be sent to author@packtpub.com. If your book idea is still at an early stage and you would like to discuss it first before writing a formal book proposal, contact us; one of our commissioning editors will get in touch with you.

We're not just looking for published authors; if you have strong technical skills but no writing experience, our experienced editors can help you develop a writing career, or simply get some additional reward for your expertise.

jQuery UI 1.8
The User Interface Library for jQuery

Build highly interactive web applications with ready-to-use widgets
from the jQuery User Interface Library

Dan Wellman

jQuery UI 1.8: The User Interface Library for jQuery

ISBN: 978-1-84951-652-5   Paperback: 424 pages

Build highly interactive web applications with ready-to-use widgets from the jQuery Interface Library

1. Packed with examples and clear explanations of how to easily design elegant and powerful front-end interfaces for your web applications

2. A section covering the widget factory including an in-depth example on how to build a custom jQuery UI widget

3. Updated code with significant changes and fixes to the previous edition

jQuery UI Themes

Create new themes for your jQuery site with this step-by-step guide

Beginner's Guide

Adam Boduch

jQuery UI Themes Beginner's Guide

ISBN: 978-1-84951-044-8   Paperback: 268 pages

Create new themes for your jQuery site with this step-by-step guide

1. Learn the details of the jQuery UI theme framework by example

2. No prior knowledge of jQuery UI or theming frameworks is necessary

3. The CSS structure is explained in an easy-to-understand and approachable way

Please check **www.PacktPub.com** for information on our titles

jQuery 1.4 Animation Techniques Beginners Guide

ISBN: 978-1-84951-330-2   Paperback: 344 pages

Quickly master all of jQuery's animation methods and build a toolkt of ready-to-use animation using jQuery 1.4

1. Create both simple and complex animations using clear, step-by-step instructions, accompanied with screenshots

2. Walk through jQuery's built-in animation methods and see in detail how each one can be used

3. Over 50 detailed examples of different types of web page animations

jQuery Hotshot

ISBN: 978-1-84951-910-6   Paperback: 296 pages

Ten practical projects that exercise your skill, build your confidence, and help you master jQuery

1. See how many of jQuery's methods and properties are used in real situations. Covers jQuery 1.9

2. Learn to build jQuery from source files, write jQuery plugins, and use jQuery UI and jQuery Mobile

3. Familiarise yourself with the latest related technologies like HTML5, CSS3, and frameworks like Knockout.js

Please check **www.PacktPub.com** for information on our titles